CORTIGIANA

(La cortigiana)
(1525)

Carleton Renaissance Plays in Translation   38

General Editors
**Donald Beecher, Carmine Di Biase,
and Massimo Ciavolella**

Marcantonio Raimondi, Portrait of Pietro Aretino, ca. 1517.

Carleton Renaissance Plays in Translation

Pietro Aretino

CORTIGIANA

Translated by
J. Douglas Campbell and Leonard G. Sbrocchi

Introduction by
Raymond B. Waddington

Dovehouse Editions Inc.
Ottawa, Canada
2003

This book has been published with the help of a grant from the Humanities and Social Sciences Federation of Canada, using funds provided by the Social Sciences and Humanities Research Council of Canada.

Canadian Cataloguing in Publication Data, National Library of Canada
Aretino, Pietro, 1492–1556
  The cortigiana / Pietro Aretino ; introduction by Raymond B. Waddington ; translation and annotations by J. Douglas Campbell and Leonard G. Sbrocchi.

(Carleton Renaissance plays in translation ; 38)
Translation of: La cortigiana.
Includes bibliographical references.

ISBN 1-895537-70-3

I. Campbell, J. Douglas, 1935–   II. Sbrocchi, Leonard G. (Leonard Gregory), 1938–   III. Title.   IV. Series.

PQ4563.C6 2003   852'.3   C2002-9003365-9

Copyright © 2003 Dovehouse Editions Inc.

For information and orders write to:
    Dovehouse Editions Inc.
    1890 Fairmeadow Cres.
    Ottawa, Canada, K1H 7B9

For information on the series:
    Carleton Renaissance Plays in Translation
    c/o Department of English
    Carleton University
    1125 Colonel By Drive
    Ottawa, Canada K1S 5B6

No part of this book may be translated or reproduced in any form, by print, photoprint, microfilm, or any other means, without written permission from the publisher.

Typeset in Canada: Carleton Production Centre

Manufactured in Canada

Front Cover: Giulio Romano, Portrait of Joanna of Aragon (given to François I by Cardinal Bibbiena in 1519).

Table of Contents

Introduction
    Pietro Aretino (1492–1556)   7
    La cortigiana in Aretino's Theatrical Achievement   9
    The Two *Cortigiana* Texts   11
    The Title   12
    La cortigiana and the *commedia erudita*   15
    Language   19
    Rome and Italy, 1517–1527   21
    The New Golden Age: Leonine Rome   24
    Castiglione's *Book of the Courtier* and *La cortigiana*   29
    Pasquino   34
    Holding the Mirror up to Nature   37
Bibliography   45

Cortigiana   49
Textual Annotations   141

Portrait of Pietro Aretino, ca. 1538.
Woodcut (after Titian?) in *I mondi del Doni*, 1552.

Introduction

Pietro Aretino (1492–1556)

Pietro was born in Arezzo, the town from which he took his name, the son of a cobbler, Luca Del Tura, and Margherita ("Tita") Bonci. In his teens, he left Arezzo for Perugia, where he may have been a student or an artist's apprentice. In 1512 he published a volume of poetry, describing himself as a painter. This combination of interests, literature and art, stayed with him throughout a life in which he became a major vernacular writer and never ceased cultivating and befriending artists. In turn, the portraits that they made for him in various media — paintings, sculpture, medals, engravings, woodcuts in his books — caused his to be the best-known face in Europe. One could accurately describe Aretino as the first media celebrity.

After leaving Perugia and passing through Siena, Aretino turned up in Rome not later than in 1517. There he established himself in the household of Agostino Chigi, a Sienese banker and reputedly the wealthiest man in Rome. By Aretino's good fortune, Chigi's villa on the Tiber, now known as the Farnesina, was in the later stages of decoration, bringing him into contact with Raphael, Giovanni da Udine, Sodoma, and Sebastiano del Piombo, and giving him *entrée* to artistic circles. Either then or later, he began writing the anonymous, satiric poems called "pasquinades" for which he would become notorious. Aretino allied himself with the Medici power structure, Pope Leo X and his nephew,

Cardinal Giulio de' Medici. When Leo died in 1521, Aretino used his pen to campaign for Giulio's election by discrediting the other candidates. This made him persona non grata upon the election of Adrian VI, causing Aretino to absent himself from Rome. The elderly Adrian lasted less than two years, however; and Giulio did win the second election, allowing Aretino's return.

The definitive image of Aretino in his second Roman tour of duty comes from Marcantonio Raimondi's engraved portrait: the dandyish, fashionably dressed courtier with elaborately combed and curled moustache and beard, wearing a soft cap with a hat badge that has been identified as a Gonzaga emblem, a reminder that Frederigo II Gonzaga was his host in exile. The face is boldly handsome, but the expression is wary, with eyes glancing to the side. He had good reason to be wary. As a hired pen, Aretino was more useful to the aspiring than the sitting pope; he earned the unforgiving enmity of Gian Matteo Giberti, the powerful papal datary; and in 1524 he involved himself in the *I modi* scandal. Aretino's artist friend, Raimondi, made a set of engravings from Giulio Romano's drawings of couples in a variety of sexual positions. In the resulting furor, the engravings were confiscated and destroyed; Giulio Romano fled from Rome, but Marcantonio Raimondi was jailed. By Aretino's own account, he helped obtain the artist's release. Then, outraged by the censorship, he composed sixteen sonnets giving voice to the figures represented in the engravings. These would have been circulated in manuscript. If an authorized edition of the engravings and sonnets was printed, it does not survive; we know them from a probably pirated, badly printed volume with crude woodcuts, which exists in a single copy. In the aftermath of the scandal, Aretino tried to smooth over relations with the pope and his datary by publishing poems praising them, and doing the same in *La cortigiana*. He may have succeeded with Clement, but not with Giberti, who ordered Aretino's assassination. The wounded poet survived the attempt on 28 July 1525, but prudently left Rome for good.[1]

After spending time in the field with his condottiere friend, Giovanni de' Medici, Aretino again took refuge in Mantua, before

---

[1] For detailed accounts of these events, see Anne Reynolds, *Renaissance Humanism at the Court of Clement* VII: *Francesco Berni's* Dialogue Against

moving in 1527 to Venice, where he settled. There Aretino formed enduring friendships with the artist Titian and the architect Jacopo Sansovino. He did not immediately throw off the mind-set of a court poet, accustomed to living by patronage; but, exhilarated by the intellectual freedom of the republic and empowered by the resources of Venice's printing industry, Aretino became the first of the *poligrafi*, the versatile writers for the vernacular press who could turn their hands to anything. In the thirties, Aretino's career took off; he continued to write verse, but prose now was his favored medium in writing satiric dialogues and prognostications, plays, biblical paraphrases, saints' lives, and, above all, letters. In 1538 he became the first vernacular writer to publish a volume of his own letters. It was an enormous success, and five more volumes followed — in all, well over 3,000 letters, an important precursor to the personal essay later developed by Montaigne.

La cortigiana in Aretino's Theatrical Achievement

Aretino's dramatic production consists of six plays: second written but first printed was *Il marescalco*, composed in Mantua (1526-27), revised and printed in Venice (1533). The Rome-written (1525) and Venice-revised *Cortigiana* came next (1534). Aretino returned to comedy in the forties, with *Lo ipocrito* (1541), *La Talanta* (1542), and *Il filosofo* (written 1544, printed 1546). Possibly seeking the respectability that attaches to more "serious" genres, he even tried his hand at a classical tragedy, the *Orazia* (1546). After a long period of neglect in English-language scholarship, *La cortigiana* belatedly has received its due. Marvin Herrick has described the *Cortigiana* and the *Marsecalco* as "among the most remarkable plays of the century."[2] Herrick commented on the 1534 edition; but, since the 1970 publication of the 1525 manuscript, criticism increasingly has discriminated the differences between the two and respected the qualities of Aretino's original version, the first

---

Poets *in Context* (New York: Garland, 1997); and Bette Talvacchia, *Taking Positions: On the Erotic in Renaissance Culture* (Princeton: Princeton University Press, 1999).

[2] Marvin T. Herrick, *Italian Comedy in the Renaissance* (Urbana: University of Illinois Press, 1960), 85. For *The Marescalco*, see the translation in this series (2nd ed., 1992).

composition to warrant careful attention. Richard Andrews calls it an "astonishing comedy," and, remarking on Aretino's influence, notes that Giordano Bruno's *Il candelaio* ('Candlebearer') "seems inspired principally by the more aggressive comedies of Aretino."[3] Aretino's anticipation of techniques developed in the *commedia dell' arte* has been recognized.[4] Indeed, appreciation for Aretino's dramatic craftsmanship and achievement as a whole perhaps now stands higher than at any time since his death. Commenting on Aretino's single tragedy, *Orazia*, Jonas Barish finds it "marked throughout by a keen feeling for stage presence, stage gesture, and stage furniture" and praises it as outdoing Corneille's tragedy *Horace* in "theatrical vividness."[5]

"Theatrical vividness" also may be the most memorable quality of the *Cortigiana* '25. Before examining that quality, however, we need to have the action clearly in mind. The comedy interlaces two plots. In the first, Messer Maco, a young fool from Siena, arrives in Rome expecting to become a cardinal, only to discover that he first must learn how to be a courtier. A street-wise Roman, Master Andrea, amuses himself giving Maco lessons before resorting to more radical measures. Maco also falls in love with a woman he has glimpsed, affording Andrea opportunities for further jokes. In the second, Parabolano, a Neapolitan who has gained a court position by dumb luck, has conceived a passion for a married woman. In desperation, he places himself in the hands of Rosso, his unscrupulous servant, who schemes with the bawd Aloigia to deceive Parabolano into thinking he has satisfied his desire. The plots are parallel in the motivations of fulfilling a master's sexual desires and in the reversals of power relations: the clever servants outwit and control the idiot masters. If one takes the court as the focal point, however, the plots are sequential. Parabolano already holds a place such as the outsider Maco hopes to attain;

---

[3] Richard Andrews, *Scripts and Scenarios: The Performance of Comedy in Renaissance Italy* (Cambridge: Cambridge University Press, 1993), 67, 243. Bruno's *Candlebearer* has been translated in this series, no. 31 (2000).

[4] See, for example, Douglas Radcliff-Umstead, *The Birth of Modern Comedy in Renaissance Italy* (Chicago: University of Chicago Press, 1969), 188.

[5] Jonas Barish, "The Problem of Closet Drama in the Italian Renaissance," *Italica* 71 (1994): 4–30; quotations 12, 16.

and Aretino devotes most attention to how his behavior affects those in his entourage.

The Two *Cortigiana* Texts

La cortigiana exists in two versions: the earlier, which was written sometime between February and July 1525, survives in a single manuscript and was not published until 1970. It is the copy text of the present translation. A revision was printed in August 1534, in Venice, by Giovanni Antonio de Nicolini da Sabio for Francesco Marcolini. The two texts differ substantially, reflecting Aretino's altered circumstances in various ways.[6] In 1525 he was a court poet, both satirizing the Roman patronage system and attempting to ingratiate himself with patrons. During the subsequent nine years, Aretino had abandoned Rome, lost his remaining Medici patron, and failed to find more than a temporary safe harbor in the court at Mantua before settling permanently in Venice and reinventing himself as the first *poligrafo*. Rome itself had endured the devastation and humiliation of the 1527 Sack by the imperial army, an event that Aretino claimed to have predicted. The topical references are changed accordingly in the *Cortigiana* of 1534; and, given the security afforded by the distance of time and place, Aretino intensified the satiric attack. The opening line of Act I, Messer Maco's statement that "Per certo che Roma è capus mundi" becomes "In fine Roma è coda mundi" — the bottom, rather than the head, of the world. When Master Andrea imparts the secrets of courtiership to Maco, in '25 he contents himself with learning how to blaspheme and to commit heresy (I, xxiv); in '34 he rattles off a list of vices, ending with "far la ninfa ed essere agente e paziente" (I, xxii) — to be a homosexual capable of taking either the active or the passive role. Other changes are indicative of Aretino's absorption in the print culture of Venice. *La cortigiana* '34 has been described as a print text conceived for readers in contrast to the performance text of '25. The later version shows more conformity to the conventions of *commedia erudita*, eliminating direct addresses to the audience for example. It also takes care to spell out physical actions for the convenience of the reader who

---

[6]For an analysis of the changes, see Paul Larivaille, *Pietro Aretino fra Rinascimento e manierismo* (Rome: Bulzoni, 1980), 123–37.

must imagine the stage scene.[7] The printing of comedies still was unusual in the thirties; not until the mid-forties did they become a common print genre, indicating their increasing acceptance as "literature." In publishing *Il marescalco* (1533) and the *Cortigiana* '34 Aretino was, in this way as well as so many others, ahead of his time in comprehending the resources and potential of the printing press. The *Cortigiana* '34 proved popular enough that it was printed a dozen times over the span of twenty years. Aretino felt so confident of his readers' familiarity with the play that, with no further identification, he quoted a line from it in his well-known "Dream of Parnassus" letter: "As Cappa said, 'Who hasn't been inside a tavern, doesn't know what Paradise is.' "[8]

Theatrically, the *Cortigiana* '25 is more boldly experimental and, in the sense of immersion in Roman life that it projects, more vivid and striking. Aretino would have circulated the play in manuscript (or, at least, intended to do so) for the amusement of his friends and the delectation of prospective patrons. Undoubtedly, he wanted the comedy to be performed. The Prologue gives reasonably explicit instructions for the *scaenae frons*, the backdrop that the audience will see when the curtain has opened: "Rome itself. Look: there's the Palace, St. Peter's, the piazza, the guards, a couple of taverns—the Hare and the Luna—the fountain, St. Catherine's—the whole thing."[9] There is no record that his ambition to see the play staged was fulfilled, however; the nearly successful assassination attempt put paid to any plans Aretino may have had for a career as a Roman court dramatist.

The Title

The term *cortigiana* is perfectly ambiguous. Used as an adjective, it means "in courtly fashion"; as a noun, it means "a courtesan," and

---

[7] As Andrews suggests, *Scripts and Scenarios*, 66–74.

[8] To Gian Iacopo Lionardi (6 December 1537, in Aretino's *Lettere*, I, no. 280). Quoted from *Aretino: Selected Letters*, trans. George Bull (Harmondsworth: Penguin, 1976), 139. In both versions of the play this is the first line of Act II.

[9] The '34 Prologue lacks this specificity. One speaker comments that Rome is unrecognizable; the other explains its condition results from the Sack.

the standard translation of the play's title has been "the courtesan." In precise usage, "courtesan" designates a *cortigiana onesta*, one of the women at the very top of the socio-commercial hierarchy of prostitution. Such women were famous for their refinement and culture; they might maintain elegantly furnished salons in which they entertained noblemen and illustrious visitors. At the farthest remove from common *meretrici*, such courtesans were literate and well read; the Venetian courtesans Veronica Franco and Gaspara Stampa were accomplished poets.[10] Although it preceded his arrival in Rome, Aretino surely would have known about the liaison between his master, Agostino Chigi, and the courtesan Imperia. Two of his *Sonetti lussuriosi* (nos. 11 and 12) refer to Roman courtesans who were prominent in the era of Leo X. Indeed, Aretino made just such a *cortigiana onesta* the title-character in his only other comedy with a Roman setting, *La Talanta* (1542).

The puzzle is that no such character appears in *La cortigiana*. The bawd Aloigia, a "bearded witch" who does a considerable line in selling love potions and cosmetic aids, claims to have been at the top of the profession in her younger days; but the boast of having worked every brothel in Italy suggests a rapid descent. Togna, the baker's wife whom Aloigia arranges to substitute for the unseen Laura, is only a part-timer, earning pocket money on the side. The fool, Messer Maco, becomes infatuated with the finely dressed "pretty lady" whom he sees at her window. It emerges that this is Camilla Pisana, an actual Roman courtesan; one of Aretino's letters reminisces about having started a brawl in her house.[11] Camilla, like Laura, exists only off-stage, hardly warranting title billing.

Recent scholars have been nearly unanimous in finding a primary reference either to courtiers or to the court itself. Suggested

---

[10] On the social hierarchy of prostitution, see Guido Ruggiero, *Binding Passions: Tales of Magic, Marriage, and Power at the End of the Renaissance* (New York: Oxford University Press, 1993), 33–56; and Margaret F. Rosenthal, *The Honest Courtesan: Veronica Franco, Citizen and Writer in Sixteenth-Century Venice* (Chicago: University of Chicago Press, 1992).

[11] See Aretino's letter to Agnolo Firenzuola, 26 October 1541, *Lettere* II, no. 301. There are some translations of Camilla's letters in Lynne Lawner, *Lives of the Courtesans: Portraits of the Renaissance* (New York: Rizzoli, 1987), 47–52.

translations include "The Courtiers' Play," "The Comedy of the Court," and "Court Affairs."[12] This emphasis highlights the play's relationship to Castiglione's *Il libro del cortegiano* ('The Book of the Courtier'), not yet published but circulated in manuscript while the author lived in Rome during the early twenties. The dual meanings of the title converge in the characterization of Roman courtiers as effeminate — *ninfa*. John Florio's Italian-English dictionary, *Queene Anne's New World of Words* (London, 1611), nicely captures both senses. A *cortegiana* is "a curtezane, a strumpet," whereas, in a definition Aretino would have approved, a *cortigiano* is "a courtier, also an Eunuch."

By metaphoric extension, "courtesan" applies to the papal court itself, which, despite the veneer of humanist learning and culture, is represented as false, corrupt, and endlessly for sale. In Pietro Bembo's dialogue, *Prose della volgar lingua* (1525), Vincenzo Calmeta, who in Castiglione's *Cortegiano* (II, 21–22) criticizes Spanish courtiers for their presumptuous manners, is himself criticized for having written that "la cortigiana lingua," the discourse used at the Roman court, is the finest of Italian dialects.[13] The court is synonymous with the city of Rome. Aretino had come to Rome in the same year that Martin Luther nailed his ninety-five theses to the church door in Wittenberg, launching the Reformation. In the rhetoric of northern Protestants, Rome always would be figured as a whore — the Scarlet Woman or Whore of Babylon (Rev. 17). In the *Cortigiana*, as Angiolina Melchiori writes, "From the very beginning, whether by opposition or by association, the reader starts to identify the binomial Rome — courtesan."[14] In a further twist, the *cortigiana* simply is theater itself. The Prologue explains that

---

[12] For these, see Giulio Ferroni, "Pietro Aretino e le corti," in *Pietro Aretino nel cinquecentenario della nascita* (Rome: Salerno, 1995), I: 26; Andrews, *Scripts and Scenarios*, 67; and Maggie Günsberg, *Gender and the Italian Stage: From the Renaissance to the Present Day* (Cambridge: Cambridge University Press, 1997), 27.

[13] See Pietro Bembo, *Prose e rime*, ed. Carlo Dionisotti (Turin: Unione Tipografico, 1960), 106–10.

[14] Angiolina Melchiori, "Emblems of Renaissance Theatre: A Study of Aretino's Comedies" (Ph.D. dissertation, Yale, 1988), 18. She analyzes the 1534 version.

the audience will witness the births and deaths of two comedies, then hastens to reassure them: "But don't be afraid, Milady Comedia Cortigiana is falser ['contrafatta'] than the chimera." Drama makes love to an audience with the expectation of payment, either in admission fees or, at the time Aretino wrote, in patronage. In the second of Aretino's dialogues about prostitutes, the experienced Nanna advises Pippa that the secret to being a successful courtesan is "Play-acting in everything you do."[15]

La cortigiana and the *commedia erudita*

Humanism was a Latin-language phenomenon, in which the study and performance of Roman "New Comedy" occupied a large part. School boys improved their Latin by acting the plays of Plautus and Terence; and, when boys became men, they continued to perform Latin comedies for learned entertainment at court, in private homes, and before literary societies. Such drama was an important element of the carnival season and similar festivals. These origins marked Italian comedy in several distinctive ways. First, unlike modern theater, which has the expectation of repeated performances, it was occasional. Although the stage scenery and the decoration of the performance room might be quite elaborate, it was all temporary. There was no purpose-built theater until well past mid-century. Actors were male (women commenced to appear on stage only in the late forties), gentleman amateurs, although it seems reasonable to suppose that professionals might be used for clown parts or a character role, such as Aloigia.

Vernacular comedy still was in its formative stage in the 1520s. The so-called "learned" (*erudita*) or "regular" (*regolare*) comedy followed the rules of ancient Roman comedy, as they were understood from Plautus and Terence and the Latin commentaries, particularly those attributed to Donatus. On such authority, they were divided into five acts and obeyed the unities of time and place. This meant that there would be a single setting, normally a particular city realistically represented by the painted back-scene, with the action taking place on the street or piazza and confined to

---

[15]See Aretino's *Dialogues*, translated by Raymond Rosenthal with epilogue by Margaret F. Rosenthal (New York: Marsilio, 1994), 217. The Italian is "e fingendo ogni tuo andamento."

a one-day or twenty-four-hour time span. The characters should be moderate in social rank, and exploit a range of stock types: young lovers, jealous husbands, foolish fathers, braggart soldiers, avaricious merchants, alluring courtesans, and the clever slave, who was easily converted to servant. The actions should be drawn from private life—love affairs and seductions, Donatus specified—and there was a fondness for double-plots, two stories intertwined or at least loosely related. Among the earlier examples, three plays in particular had a marked influence on Aretino.

Ariosto's *I suppositi* (1508) was performed at the ducal court in Ferrara (6 February 1509) and, a decade later (6 March 1519), in Rome before Leo X, in the Vatican apartments of the pope's nephew, Cardinal Cibo. By modern standards, Rome still was a small city of perhaps 55,000, and literary circles were tight. Raphael, who only the year before had completed his work at Agostino Chigi's villa, created the scene, a backdrop of Ferrara in perspective. Aretino was then a member of Chigi's household, where he became acquainted with Raphael. A decade or so later, when Ariosto rewrote the prose comedy in verse, he joked about the *Modi* scandal, in which Aretino had involved himself.[16] *I suppositi*, which later was translated into English by George Gascoigne (1566) and provided one plot for *The Taming of the Shrew*, exploits the devices that rapidly became standard in this genre. Ariosto's Prologue states forthrightly: "It is called the *Pretenders* because it is full of substitutions and pretense." Moreover, the play gave Aretino a useful precedent for set speeches and monologues of social commentary—attacks on lawyers and customs officials, opinions on the Turkish threat—that do not advance the action.

Second, Bernardo Dovizi, called "Bibbiena," was known for his love of *beffe*, practical jokes, which caused Castiglione to assign to him the discourse on humor in *The Book of the Courtier* (Book II). Bibbiena wrote *La Calandra* (or *Calandria*), which was performed at the court of Urbino during the 1513 carnival season, and Castiglione wrote a prologue for it. The comedy then was performed at Rome in 1514 and 1515 for Leo X, a man fond of a good joke, who

---

[16] On the Roman performance, see *The Comedies of Ariosto*, ed. and trans. Edmond M. Beame and Leonard G. Sbrocchi (Chicago: University of Chicago Press, 1975), xxvi; and 95, n. 1, for the Prologue to the verse play.

had promoted the author from apostolic protonotary to treasurer of his household to cardinal. Raphael painted Bibbiena's portrait, as well as frescoes for his bathroom (1516). Set in Rome, *La Calandra* draws on Plautus' *Menaechmi* for the device of identical twins, and introduces the enduring conventions of cross-dressing (girl disguised as boy, boy disguised as girl) and the bed trick. Two characters, a foolish pedant and a magician-con man, would become popular types. A central action involves the gulling of a fool derived from Boccaccio, Dr. Calandro; it postulates the primary motivation of sexual appetite and, with much bawdy innuendo, celebrates the triumph of adultery.

Third, Machiavelli's *Mandragola* (1518?) was performed in Florence with such success that Leo X insisted on having the same actors and scenery for a command performance in the spring of 1520. Both Raphael and Agostino Chigi died, within days of each other, in April of that year. Aretino may already have shifted his services to the pope, and it is quite possible that he witnessed this performance. Although the *Mandragola* is distinctive in having a single plot, in many ways it extends the themes and devices of *La Calandra*. Like Bibbiena, Machiavelli projects an amoral society animated by greed and lust; disguise and deception propel the plot to triumphant adultery. In this version of the bed trick, the foolish husband arranges the substitution that cuckolds him, whereas the undeceived wife colludes with her seducer.

The element of mordant satire on clerical corruption caught Aretino's attention. Act III, scene xvi of the *Cortigiana*, in which Aloigia consults the Father Guardian of Araceli, echoes Act III, scene iii of the *Mandagola*, a conversation between Friar Timoteo and an unnamed woman: both women seek reassurance about the purgatorial state of a dead loved one; both are anxious about the possibility of a Turkish invasion and, with obvious sexual innuendo, the consequent "impalement." Aretino's scene, more elaborate than Machiavelli's, has been described both as imitation and as parody; and, certainly, he was fond of parodying authors whom he admired.[17] One might understand the scene as functioning like the modern cinematic *hommages* to Alfred Hitchcock

---

[17] For one analysis of these scenes, see Maristella de Panizza Lorch, "Confessore e chiesa in tre commedie del Rinascimento: 'Philogenia,'

by which young directors acknowledge a formative influence and pay their respects.

Aretino's attitude toward the rules of "regular" comedy has frequently been adduced from the Prologue, spoken by two actors (*istrioni*), which opens with a sharp intimation of comedy-turned-upside-down. Histrion I, throwing up his hands at the entire notion of a prologue, advises the audience to skip the whole performance, just *plaudite et valete* ('applaud and go home'). The Latin phrase is the customary formula for the epilogue of Roman comedy. Histrion II concludes the "Argomento" or plot summary with a swagger: "don't fret," he commands, if you see actors making too many entrances or speaking out of character, "this isn't Athens: they do things differently here." If that's not clear enough, we are told that the author "has a mind of his own." The emphatic attacks on New Comedy conventions can be misleading, however.

The play itself is divided into the canonical five acts (if with an unusual number of scenes) and maintains, at least loosely, the unities of place and time. The action occupies a morning-to-midnight span, and it occurs on the streets of Rome, before several houses (if ranging quite widely through the city). Although Aretino rejects the prevailing Terentian convention by allowing his characters to speak directly to the audience, this is a matter of choosing the alternative, Plautine convention.[18] Despite the overt rebellion against the rules, this comedy probably conforms to expectations as much as it violates them. In this, *Cortigiana* '25 is a trial run for an authorial attitude that Aretino would refine and repeat constantly in his non-dramatic prose: one should imitate nature and life, rejecting the pedantry of humanists, classicism, and the clichés of Petrarchism. In fact, as his unerring satire demonstrates, Aretino had a thorough knowledge and sophisticated understanding of the high literary culture that he overtly dismisses while using whatever parts of it that suit him.

'Mandragola,' e 'Cortigiana,'" in *Il teatro italiano del Rinascimento*, ed. Maristella de Panizza Lorch (Milan: Edizioni di Comunità, 1980), 301–48.

[18]On this, see Richard Andrews, "Rhetoric and Drama: Monologues and Set Speeches in Aretino's Comedies," in *The Languages of Literature in Renaissance Italy*, ed. Peter Hainsworth et al. (Oxford: Clarendon, 1988), 158, who notes four instances, aside from the Prologue.

Later in the Prologue, Histrion I gives a rather precise statement of the combination in this comedy, "Her father's from Tuscany and her mother's from Bergamo." Literally, her father, Aretino, was, indeed, from Tuscany. Figuratively, however, Tuscany embodied the "classical" tradition of Italian literature—the Holy Trinity of Dante, Petrarch, and Boccaccio—and the approved standard of Italian literary language, for which Pietro Bembo would argue in his treatise of the same year. Conversely, Bergamo was proverbial for an uncouth country dialect and perhaps already associated with an improvisatory street theater that two decades later evolved into the *commedia dell' arte*. The wedding of Tuscan to Bergomask, then, epitomizes the combination of elements at work in the play.

Language

Ariosto's first two comedies *La cassaria* and *I suppositi* were written in vernacular prose and later rewritten in verse, and published in that form after his death. This procedure would have seemed less unusual then than it does now. The "translation" of Latin prose to verse or verse to prose was a familiar exercise set for schoolboys by their humanist masters. Ariosto may have intended the prose versions as scripts for actors and felt that printed texts deserved the dignity of verse. If so, he was swimming against the tide. There is an extensive literature on the "questione della lingua," the debate between the humanists committed to Latin and those who argued for the legitimacy of the vernacular. Pietro Bembo's *Prose della volgar lingua* (1525) arbitrated by approving the use of vernacular, but insisting on a standard of "classical" Tuscan as it was used by fourteenth-century writers. Theatrical practice, however, already had embraced a contemporary, idiomatic Italian, as *La Calandra* and *La mandragola* demonstrate. The Prologue of *La cortigiana*, perhaps not coincidentally in the same year as Bembo's dialogue, stands as a counter-manifesto.

Histrion I offers a comic myth of origins to assert the case for linguistic freedom and diversity. "Look how many languages there are to be read," he insists, explaining that Pasquino, the genius of Roman satire, was born of a liaison between an unknown poet and one of the Muses. The bastard was gifted with the entire range of languages spoken by the nine Muses: "sometimes he speaks

Greek, sometimes Corsican, or French, or German, Bergamask, Genoese, Venetian, Neapolitan." As for spoken Italian, Histrion I gives examples of the differing vocabulary in Tuscan, Milanese, and Bolognese.

Histrion II expresses his disgust and boredom with the long-winded speech; the play, nonetheless, bears out the praise of linguistic diversity. Messer Maco comes from Siena, which, like Bergamo, was known for its country dialect; but he has been a student, so drops the odd Latin phrase into his conversation and wrings out atrocious Petrarchan poems for Camilla Pisana. Parabolano, on the other hand, is a Neapolitan and mixes Spanish vocabulary with his Italian. Since 1504, the kingdom of Naples had been ruled by a Spanish viceroy, and the play records the Spanish presence increasingly evident in Rome. Parabolano's trickster servant, Rosso, cheats a fishmonger, who is a Florentine, and Romanello, the Jewish clothing vendor, providing opportunity for a range of dialects and accents, as does Master Andrea's joke of disguising Maco as a Sicilian porter. Other characters offer a range of diction, from high to low or, always a feature of city life, the specialized vocabularies of trades and professions. Histrion I comments dryly that, before the curtain went up, "you probably thought it was the Tower of Babel back there, but instead it was Rome itself." Rome was a melting pot, and the language of the play realistically reflects this.

Aretino had a remarkable ear for regional and dialectic difference and for the expressive range of social registers within any given type of speech, whether Tuscan, Roman, or Venetian.[19] Moreover, his earlier training in poetry enhanced his facility in recreating the varieties of spoken Italian on paper. The most distinctive trait of his writing is linguistic exuberance; for a poetic analogue, one might think of Walt Whitman or Wallace Stevens. Lists, catalogues, names, sequences of alternative figures of speech are characteristic devices conveying his delight in the cornucopia

---

[19]See Luciana Zampolli, "La retorica in commedia: aspetti linguistici del teatro comico di Pietro Aretino," in *Scenery, Set and Staging in the Italian Renaissance: Studies in the Practice of Theatre*, ed. Christopher Cairns (Lewiston: Edwin Mellen, 1996), 136–79 (with English summary), to whom I am indebted for some points in this paragraph.

of language. Facility in copiousness, the orator's resourcefulness in never running out of words, was a heritage of Ciceronian rhetoric, the stock-in-trade of Renaissance humanists. Erasmus, whom Aretino admired and from whose work he learned a great deal, once enumerated 147 different ways of saying, "I was glad to get your letter." Aretino extended the boundaries of Latin *copia*, first, by inventiveness, including a taste for neologisms. Writing at the end of the century, John Florio wondered, "How then ayme we at *Peter Aretine*, that is so wittie, hath such varietie, and frames so manie new words?"[20] Second, notoriously, Aretino extended the range to language from the streets and the bordellos, including a command of vulgarities and obscenities unprecedented in print. Histrion I describes the union that produced Pasquino as "alchemy" (*archimia*); the objective of this popular pseudo-science was the transmutation of base metals into gold, a fitting metaphor for Aretino's own skill in creating literature from a sub-literary vocabulary. Although less conspicuously, he is nearly as good with the upper range. In *La cortigiana*, Petrarchan cliches and bits of Latin, often church Latin, signal pretentiousness and vacuity or moral bankruptcy, whereas the melange of colloquial Spanish terms with Italian suggests the disintegration of Roman society.

Rome and Italy, 1517–27

During his time in Rome, Aretino lived under two popes, Leo X and Clement VII, discreetly vanishing during Adrian VI's brief tenure. Since Rome was the dominant factor in the Italian political situation, some historical review may be helpful. Italy was slower than most western European countries in making the transition from a feudal political organization, remaining a collection of city-states — whether republics, oligarchies, or papal clients — at a time when France, Spain, and England were evolving into nations and, eventually, absolutist states. Indeed, Italy did not become a modern, unified country until 1871. The economy contributed to the stagnant situation in the sixteenth century. Improved navigational instruments, advances in ship building, and new weapons technology made possible extended trade routes and New World colonization. This had the effect of shifting merchant economy

---

[20]Florio, *A Worlde of Wordes* (London, 1598), "Epistle dedicatorie."

from the Mediterranean to the Atlantic; consequently, trade was slow and the financial resources of the peninsula were generally in decline. At the same time, the expanding Ottoman Empire was gaining control of the eastern Mediterranean. By 1526 the Turks, led by Suleiman the Magnificent, had overrun Hungary and captured Budapest. A decade earlier, raiders had swooped down on towns near the mouth of the Tiber, carrying off prisoners and narrowly missing the pope himself.[21] Aloigia's anxiety about "impalement" by the Turks is not totally far-fetched.

Throughout this period, the Kingdom of Naples was in Spanish control; effectively, southern Italy was a Spanish fiefdom. Spain's presence in Rome had been prominent ever since the Borgia (originally Borja) popes, Calixtus III (1455–58) and the feared Alexander VI (1492–1503); the sixteenth century witnessed the city's transformation into "Spanish Rome."[22] The effects of the Spanish invasion are evident in the comedy: Aloigia mocks their manners (V, xiv), but, when Master Andrea and Zoppino become bored with their joke and beat Maco from Camilla's bedroom, he has no doubt about who is responsible: "The Spaniards wounded me! Thieves! Animals! Scoundrels!" (V, xxi). Maco's mistaken, but understandable, assumption is consistent with the accounts of the Sack of Rome, which agree that the Spanish were the most merciless of the assailants, outdoing the German and Italian mercenaries in cruelty.[23]

In the second and third decades of the century, Northern Italy became a battleground between France and Spain. A precarious independence was maintained by the republics, Venice and intermittently Florence, whereas a lack of independence occasionally gained a measure of security for the Papal States subservient to Rome. Leo X proved to be an unexpectedly adroit card-player, using a bewildering sequence of shifting alliances, treaties, negotiations, and betrayals to maintain a balance of power between

---

[21] For this episode, see Bonner Mitchell, *Rome in the High Renaissance: The Age of Leo X* (Norman: University of Oklahoma Press, 1973), 31.

[22] See Thomas James Dandelet, *Spanish Rome: 1500–1700* (New Haven: Yale University Press, 2001).

[23] See Dandelet, 37.

France and Spain, thereby preventing either from gaining a dominance that would render Rome helpless. Adrian's reign was too brief to have any real effect, but Clement's vacillating indecisiveness and belated bad choices proved fatal.

Spain's dominance became complete in 1525 with the defeat and capture of Francis I at the battle of Pavia, bringing down the house of cards that Leo had constructed. The street vendor of broadsides and pamphlets (I, iv) advertises current news with "The Peace between Christianity and the Emperor! The Capture of the King!" The king, of course, is Francis I, captured on 25 February; and the late-breaking news, getting top billing, probably refers to the treaty of 1 April, between Clement and Charles de Lannoy, viceroy of Naples, pledging the pope and emperor to mutual aid. Unfortunately for Clement, Charles V was not so easily satisfied. He did not forgive Clement for signing a secret alliance with Francis (December 1524) while professing loyalty to the emperor; when Clement joined the League of Cognac (May 1526) against Charles, it was the last straw.

Charles commissioned a new army composed largely of German mercenaries, many of them Lutherans, and Spanish regulars. The only loyal condottiere capable of repelling the invasion was Aretino's friend and protector, Giovanni de' Medici (called Giovanni delle Bande Nere); unluckily, Giovanni received a fatal wound in an early skirmish with the Germans. Recognizing his inability to hold off the imperial army, Clement made yet another treaty with Lannoy; in the belief that the field commanders would honor the terms of the peace treaty, Clement, disastrously, dismissed the troops guarding Rome itself. He had failed to understand that the under-funded army, promised payment in plunder, was by this point an uncontrollable force.

The Sack of Rome itself began on 6 May 1527 and continued for eight days; Clement, having taken refuge in the Castel Sant' Angelo, remained imprisoned there until December; the city itself remained occupied until February 1528.[24] In European

---

[24] On the Sack, see, for example, Massimo Firpo, *Il Sacco di Roma del 1527: Tra profezia, propaganda politica e riforma religiosa* (Cagliari, 1990); and André Chastel, *The Sack of Rome, 1527*, trans. Beth Archer (Princeton: Princeton University Press, 1983).

consciousness the Sack was felt as a catastrophe. Contemporaries, remembering Rome's mythic origin as the new Troy, viewed the devastation inflicted on the city as a second fall of Troy, and the horrors suffered by its inhabitants were readily figured as the rape of Rome herself. Aretino later exploited both tropes to describe the Sack in one of his dialogues about prostitutes, *Dialogo nel quale la Nanna . . . insegna a la Pippa* (1536).[25] Charles V, shocked by the extent of the devastation and the barbarous cruelty of the imperial army, disclaimed responsibility for the Sack; his secretary, Alfonso de Valdes, wrote a dialogue arguing that the luxury and corruption of the Roman curia provoked the soldiers to such atrocities. Writing an open letter to Clement less than a month after the Sack, Aretino advised him that "the will of God" caused his misfortunes "because of the sins and vices of the clergy."[26] Clement himself gloomily took a similar view in a Palm Sunday sermon (1528). Marin Sanudo recorded in his diary the report that "the pope exhorted the cardinals and prelates to alter their ways, to do penance for their sins, for that was what caused the scourge (*il flagello*) that befell Rome."[27]

The New Golden Age: Leonine Rome

In the Middle Ages, Rome had been a provincial backwash, with flocks of sheep grazing among the ruins of antiquity; for most of the fourteenth century the pope resided in Avignon. Even when the papal curia returned to the Eternal City, Florence, not Rome, was the intellectual and cultural center of the early Renaissance. But by the beginning of the sixteenth century the *renovatio urbis* was well under way and all this was changing. Extensive new building projects were launched, jostling incongruously among the medieval structures; the grandeur that had been classical Rome

---

[25] See *Aretino's Dialogues*, 240–53, for a travesty of Virgil's *Aeneid*, IV; and page 267 for gang rape. The latter has been discussed by James Grantham Turner in "The Sack of Rome as Pornography in Aretino and his Followers," a paper given at the 2001 Renaissance Society of America meeting.

[26] Quoted from *Aretino: Selected Letters*, 61–63.

[27] Quoted from Chastel, 185.

was rediscovered; popes adopted an imperial style;[28] humanists, artists, poets, and every category of lesser mortal flocked to the city.

The paradoxes and incongruities that characterized this new Golden Age of Rome were embodied in its pope, Leo X.[29] Giovanni, the second son of Lorenzo de' Medici, received a brilliant humanist education, became a cardinal at fourteen, and, when he went to Rome, charmed everyone with his gracious and modest personality, his generosity, his cultivation of the arts. Elected to succeed Julius II in 1513, he was supposed to have said, "Let us enjoy the papacy, since God has given it to us." The story contains, at least, a poetic truth. Leo was a fat man in poor health, yet an avid hunter. Elected to be a peace-maker who emulated the *pax Romana* of Augustus, he exhausted the treasury in an unpopular war against Urbino. Despite his famous good nature, he ruthlessly punished conspirators who had plotted his assassination, and lost no opportunity to prefer members of the Medici family. A collector of fine arts, a devotee of music and theater, a patron of artists such as Raphael, and an intellectual who sponsored Greek studies, Leo nonetheless gathered buffoons and dwarves for amusement and liked nothing so much as a good practical joke.

The Prologue to the *Cortigiana* alludes to a famous example in which a bad poet was mounted on Hanno, the elephant that the king of Portugal had given to Leo, and led in procession to the Capitoline Hill for a mock coronation. Whatever pleased Leo, he rewarded lavishly. Fra Mariano Fetti, Leo's favorite buffoon, was appointed keeper of the papal seal (*Piombatore*), and sufficiently well compensated that he had a villa with gardens on the fashionable Quirinale Hill and commissioned religious paintings.[30]

---

[28] For the pope as caesar, see Charles L. Stinger, *The Renaissance in Rome* (Bloomington, Ind.: Indiana University Press, 1985), 238–46.

[29] On the extensive use of the Golden Age trope, see Stinger, 296–99. See further Ingrid D. Rowland, *The Culture of the High Renaissance: Ancients and Moderns in Sixteenth-Century Rome* (Cambridge: Cambridge University Press, 1998), 211–44; and Mitchell, *Rome in the High Renaissance*.

[30] See Cynthia Stollhans, "Fra Mariano, Peruzzi and Polidoro da Caravaggio: A New Look at Religious Landscapes in Renaissance Rome," *Sixteenth Century Journal* 23 (1992): 506–25.

Offsetting Leo the amiable aesthete was the Machiavellian politician who deviously played Spain against France to protect the papal states, and replenished his depleted treasury by creating and selling new offices, including thirty-seven cardinals in 1517, the year Aretino arrived. In Guicciardini's judicious assessment, Leo was "A Prince in whom were many things worthy of praise and great blame; one who greatly failed to fulfill the expectations that had been aroused by his assumption to the pontificate, since he governed with much more prudence but much less goodness than everyone had foreseen."[31]

Erasmus visited Rome in 1509, as did Martin Luther a year later. However much they differed on matters of religion, the impressions they carried away have a strong congruence: worldliness, paganism, and immorality. For Luther, Rome was "more corrupt than either Babylon or Sodom."[32] Eramus's *Ciceronianus* (1528) makes it evident that he regarded the imitation of a sterile Ciceronian style as only symptomatic of a pervasive embracing of pagan attitudes. The creeping paganism that Erasmus so deplored could be exemplified by Raphael's assimilation of the grotesque style from the Roman wall paintings in the Domus Aurea to such projects as the frescoes for the loggetta of the Vatican. Maco, dutifully trying to learn about Roman antiquity, inquires, "But must all antiquities be grottoes?" (I, xxiv). Luther, on the other hand, may have been more troubled by another recovery from antiquity: the toleration of homosexuality and pederasty. The humanist secretaries and clerks who staffed the bureaucracy of the Roman curia, as well as the circles of *letterati*, adopted "Socratic love" as a fashionable style. Aretino's Histrion I, trying to quiet the noisy audience, threatens to tell, in good humanist Latin, "el tal è agens, el tal è patiens" ('which of you are the active and which the passive sodomites'). Sure to draw a knowing laugh, the language here defines a class as the satiric target; since he does not follow through on the threat, no individual can be offended.

La cortigiana supplies a profile of Roman society under the Medici popes. The phrases "Roman court" and "Curia Romana"

---

[31] Francesco Guicciardini, *The History of Italy*, ed. and trans. Sidney Alexander (Princeton: Princeton University Press, 1984), 328.

[32] Quoted from Mitchell, 107.

describe the papal household, which included the pope's domestic prelates, the College of Cardinals, some administrative units such as offices of the datary (under Clement, Aretino's enemy, Gian Matteo Giberti), and a large number of "familiars" who were permanent members of the papal household. Under Leo the number of "familiars" and their servants rose to approximately 700, whereas the household itself employed about 2,000 people.[33] Subordinate to the curia and much weaker was the civic government, "Senatus Populus Que Romanis" or "S.P.Q.R." Leo, the adroit politician, won the enthusiastic support of the city government by having it confer Roman citizenship on his brother and nephew in a spectacular two-day public pageant.

That honor placed Giuliano and Lorenzo de' Medici among a distinct minority; a census conducted in 1526-27 indicates that only about a quarter of the city's inhabitants were native Romans. The majority, nearly sixty percent, came from other regions of Italy and the remainder were foreigners.[34] Rome was a city to which people migrated, hoping to make their fortunes. Aretino represents Parabolano as the one insider who has made it to the papal household, "at court more through the whim of fortune than through his own merits" (Prologue). As such, he has his own courtiers, Flaminio and Valerio, as well as lesser servants, Rosso and Cappa. Maco has come from Siena, with his own servants Sanese and Grillo, hoping to become a courtier and rise to a cardinal, but also fills the role of a tourist.

Aside from papal administration, Rome's main business was catering to the needs of pilgrims and tourists; then as now the city flourished as a service economy. Virtually every other character fills a niche in the service infrastructure. People must be fed — whether by Ercolano, baker for the papal household, Faccenda, the fishmonger, or simply a convenient tavern (II, i) — and clothed, here by the Jewish vendor, Romanello.[35] Health and

---

[33]See Peter Partner, *Renaissance Rome 1500–1559: A Portrait of a Society* (Berkeley: University of California Press, 1976), 117–18; and Stinger, 27–28.

[34]See the analysis by Partner, 75–76.

[35]Although the Jewish population of Rome (estimated at 1,700) was treated reasonably well by contemporary standards, those standards were

personal well-being are maintained by the remedies of Master Mercurio and those Aloigia has inherited from Lady Maggiorina, whereas the parish priest, here the Father Guardian of Araceli, sees to spiritual well-being. Current news is provided by the vendor of broadsides and pamphlets, who represents Rome's active printing industry. Visitors and residents alike also require recreation, which is provided by taverns, such as the Hare and the Luna (Prologue); by the tobacconist Zoppino; and — at the high and low ends of the spectrum — by the courtesan Camilla Pisana, the bawd Aloigia, and Togna, the willing wife of Ercolano. Even the Father Guardian concedes that "we [priests] know how to get what we want, too — whether it's a bit of veal or a young goat" (III, xvi). His expression suggests a taste for altar boys and young seminarians.[36]

The sexual licence of Medicean Rome may have been most visible in prostitution; certainly, literary accounts make much of it. In this respect, Aretino's name has been persistently linked with that of Francisco Delicado, author of the picaresque dialogue, *Retrato de la Lozana andaluza*.[37] Delicado was born into a *converso* family that fled Spain with the 1492 expulsion of the Jews, and resettled in the Rome of Julius II, where Francisco entered religious orders. He remained there until February 1528, when, in the wake of the Sack, he fled to Venice, and published *La Lozana andaluza* in the same year. Delicado does have suggestive associations with Aretino: *La Lozana* was printed by Giovanni Antonio Nicolini da Sabbio, who, in 1534–37, printed seven Aretino titles. In the period 1531–34, Delicado worked as *editore e correttore* on several Spanish-language books. In the close-knit community of Venetian authors

far from modern. See Partner, 100–02; and Mitchell, 45–50, who comments on the Romanello episode.

[36] See Valter Boggione and Giovanni Casalegno, *Dizionario storico del lessico erotico italiano* (Milan: Longanei, 1996), s.v.

[37] See, for example, Mitchell, 54–55; Partner, 99–100; Bruno M. Damiani, *Francisco Delicado* (New York: Twayne, 1974), 110–18; and, most extensively, Louis Imperiale, *La Roma clandestina de Francisco Delicado y Pietro Aretino* (New York: Peter Lang, 1997). There is an English translation of the Spanish text. See Delicado, *Portrait of Lozana, The Lusty Andalusian Woman*, trans. Bruno M. Damiani (Potomac, Md., 1987).

and printers the likelihood that Aretino was aware of Delicado and his work is strong.

Delicado's handling of fictive narrative in dialogue form seems rudimentary when compared to Aretino's; but there are tantalizing resemblances between Lozana's career from courtesan to prostitute-cum-bawd and the life of Nanna in Aretino's 1534 and 1536 dialogues, not to mention both authors' use of realistically low vocabulary and almost sociological descriptions of ordinary Roman life. Aretino may well have absorbed *La Lozana* in the process of crafting his *Ragionamenti*. Nonetheless, the equation of Rome with prostitution is less overt in *La cortigiana* than in the Nanna dialogues. Rather, the courtesan metaphor hovers at large, while the specific concerns of the comedy are closer to those in a later dialogue, the *Ragionamento delle corti* (1538): ambition, greed, pretense, dishonesty, hypocrisy.[38] Histrion II states plainly that the plots are contrived to permit the audience to "witness a small sampling of the courtly ways ['costumi cortigiani'] of men and women."

Castiglione's *Book of the Courtier* and *La cortigiana*

Baldasarre Castiglione (1478–1529) spent most of his life as a courtier, sometimes in military service but largely in diplomacy. From 1504 to 1516 he served successive Dukes of Urbino, representing the duchy at Rome for three years. He entered service with the Duke of Mantua in 1519, frequently as emissary to the papal court; in 1524 Clement VII sent him to Spain as papal nuncio to the imperial court. He remained there until his death from plague in 1529; the emperor, Charles V, mourned him as one of the greatest courtiers in the world. Castiglione completed the first version of his most famous literary work by 1516, revised it, and in 1518 sent manuscript copies to friends for their advice. This generated further revisions during the early twenties; he continued to revise in Spain, until, fearing that one of the manuscript copies in circulation might be pirated, he sent the book to Venice, where it was printed in 1528. Aretino may well have met Castiglione in

---

[38] The best discussion of this dialogue remains that by Amedeo Quondam, "La scena della menzogna: corte e cortigiano nel 'Ragionamento' di Pietro Aretino," *Psicon*, nos. 8–9 (1978): 4–23.

Rome through Raphael or another of his contacts. He certainly knew about the book, and details of his parodies in several works suggest that he had access to an intermediate manuscript version.

In its final form, *The Book of the Courtier* is a dialogue in four books with connecting narrative, set in the ducal palace at Urbino in March 1507. The participants are four women and nineteen men, all real persons. The custom being to gather for conversation after dinner, it is proposed "to fashion in words a perfect courtier, setting forth all the conditions and particular qualities requisite for a man deserving of this name." The game continues over four nights, with one or two principal speakers in each and the others freely adding, contradicting, or qualifying their accounts. The first night sets forth the Courtier's natural prerequisites (birth, intelligence, appearance), physical skills, and social graces. The second night continues with various practical considerations before shifting to an analysis of humor. Book III addresses the qualities of a perfect lady and her role in relation to the courtier. The last night considers the purpose of the courtier's perfection, which is not an end in itself but a means of better serving his prince, before examining the qualities of the ideal prince and the merits of different political systems. In closing, it returns to the courtier's private life with a definition of love and its proper purpose. Several key words emerge early in the dialogue: the courtier should do everything with grace (*grazia*), and cultivate the art of seeming to do everything artlessly, effortlessly, with nonchalance (*sprezzatura*). Above all, the courtier must avoid affectation (*affettazione*).

The satire that Aretino directs against *The Courtier* is overt and broad in the Maco plot. Master Andrea assures Maco that he cannot achieve his goal of becoming a cardinal without first being a courtier, offering his own service as tutor: "I'll get you the book that teaches the art of courtier-making." When Andrea goes off to fetch the book, Maco impatiently orders his servant Sanese to buy a copy from a street-vendor (whose stock, ominously, includes *The Failed Courtier*); the barely literate Sanese is cheated with the wrong book. Andrea eventually returns with the right book and gives the first lesson, on learning how to blaspheme and commit heresy (I, xxiv).

The satire is not a point-by-point reversal of Castiglione; much of it is focused on Book II. The germ of the entire Maco plot may have emerged from the account of politically favored dullards who must be extravagantly praised to their faces while everyone laughs behind their backs (II, 32). Some dolts, thinking themselves witty, speak indecently and behave boorishly with ladies (II, 36), as Maco certainly does to Camilla's maid (V, iv), persistently failing to make the requisite good first impression. Castiglione's speakers expatiate on the appropriate style of dress and manner of walking (II, 27–28); when Andrea attempts to teach Maco the mannerisms of a duke (II, ii), his pupil succeeds only in falling down. Poor Maco constantly parades his learning with incorrect or inappropriate Latin tags; his poetry in Latin or Italian causes Andrea excruciating pain (I, xxix, II, xii), as does his Petrarchan love letter (II, xi); he recognizes that a courtier should be skilled in music, but confuses that word with *mosaic* (II, vii). Whereas it is unseemly for a courtier to put on a peasant's clothing (II, 50), Maco is dressed in a porter's costume and comes to believe that his identity has been stolen.

Such pinpricks of satire are less memorable, however, than Aretino's grander flights of invention. Although Andrea had advertised the effectiveness of "the book" in the metaphor of Ovidian metamorphosis, turning "beasts into men," when he tires of the instruction jokes, he tells Maco that he must be reshaped in the "mold" that makes courtiers and does so by dunking him in a cauldron of hot water. The shift from comic tutorial to physical humor (albeit narrated, not presented on stage) actually turns on Aretino's delight in the shiftiness of language: *per le forme* means 'according to the forms' — i.e., by the book. But, equally, 'forms' could mean 'molds,' such as those in which hats were made by the steaming of felt.[39] Literally, Maco is to be reformed, and the unrelenting Andrea shows him his reflection in a mirror to convince him that it has happened. At the same time the fraudulent doctor, Mercurio, persuades Maco that he must take "pills" (actually medlars that make him sick) to complete the transformation. The tricks are more evocative of Aristophanes than anything related to the realistic conventions of New Comedy; and certainly they convey Aretino's derision of the simple-minded notion that Castiglione's dialogue could be used as a handbook for training courtiers, as if they could be shaped in a mold.

---

[39] As Andrews, *Scripts and Scenarios*, 255, n. 12, has pointed out.

Less obvious but no less deadly is the treatment of Parabolano, the recently elevated lord, who constitutes an "after" to Maco's "before." He is the embodiment of affectation, the worst fault in a courtier's behavior (I, 27). Cappa, who can remember when his master was a mere stable boy, is outraged by the airs that Parabolano now has adopted: "the bastard has a servant use a silver tray to bring him the paper to wipe his ass with — and before he takes it the servant has to bow to him" (I, ix). Parabolano's current affectation, adopting the mannerisms of a fashionable melancholy lover, follows from his delusion that he is in love with the unseen and appropriately Petrarchan "Laura," providing an opportunity for the rogue servant Rosso to advance himself while abusing his master. Parabolano also has in his service two honest courtiers, Flaminio and Valerio, who, although completely aware of their master's folly and gullibility, are genuinely concerned for his welfare. Valerio gives Parabolano candid advice concerning his infatuation and repeatedly warns him of Rosso's duplicity; he only gets sacked for his pains. So much for the courtier's primary responsibility of advising his prince honestly and leading him on the path of virtue (IV, 5–10). Aretino flexibly uses Castiglione both pro and con; he mocks the attributes of the ideal courtier, but willingly uses good courtiers to highlight bad masters.

The most celebrated part of *The Courtier* is Pietro Bembo's Book IV speech on Platonic love, which, he explains, should function as a ladder: the beloved's physical beauty should lead one to appreciate her spiritual beauty; since her soul is a spark of Divine Beauty, one should progress from the individual to desire for that ultimate, intangible Beauty. The only ladders in *La cortigiana*, however, are instruments of self-love and social advancement. When the ambitious Rosso, pretending to be a nobleman, tricks the fishmonger, he tells him — revealingly — that his coat of arms is "a golden ladder on a blue field." His real master, Parabolano, reflects, "When I was a nobody, the itch to climb the ladder bothered me twenty-four hours a day." Now Parabolano is tormented even more by the itch of love. Although Bembo allows that it is more forgivable in young men to get stuck on the first step of the ladder and succumb to "sensual love," the awkwardness with which both would-be lovers seek to alleviate the itch is decidedly anti-Platonic. Maco explains that he only had undressed to go to

INTRODUCTION 33

bed with Camilla, when he was attacked by "the Spaniards" (actually Andrea and Zoppino) and forced to jump out the window in his nightshirt. Parabolano is more humiliatingly successful; after consummating the act, he discovers that he has gone to bed not with Laura but with Togna, the wife of the palace baker, a crushing blow to his vanity. Unlike Maco, however, Parabolano is capable of learning. As the victim of the practical joke in which a man tricks himself (II, 87), he recognizes that he can defuse the joke by accepting it with good grace. He reinstates Valerio, forgives Aloigia, reconciles Ercolano to Togna, and, to better enjoy the fun, wants it all made into a comedy.

Parabolano's determination "to see all discord resolved at my expense" by having the "witty and well read" Bartolomeo Pattolo shape the story of all the night's jokes at his own, Ercolano's, and Maco's expense into a *commedia erudita* signals a change that moves in the right direction, but he still has much to learn. If he admires Pattolo, a poetaster at Leo X's court, he remains a fool. Valerio, perhaps having himself learned the need for tact, obliquely nudges him toward a better choice; in his virtuoso speech to Ercolano on the honor of having horns he mentions the coat of arms of Cardinal Bibbiena, author of *La Calandra* and a superior playwright.

Book II of *The Courtier* offers the thesis that the courtier should bring "gaiety and laughter" to people with his "amusing witticisms and pleasantries." Given the task of discoursing on the art of humor, Castiglione's friend Bibbiena, in a section loosely modelled on the discussion of humor in Cicero's *De oratore*, divides jokes into three categories: urbane or festive narratives, brief witticisms, and practical jokes (*burle* or *beffe*). The last themselves are subdivided into several types that are suggestive like those in the *Cortigiana*. Parabolano falls victim to the kind in which "a net is spread, as it were, and a little bait is put out, so that a man easily tricks himself" (II, 85). Maco falls victim to that "wherein someone is cleverly deceived in a fine and amusing manner"; and Bibbiena's example of the man who is convinced by his companions that he suddenly has gone blind (II, 86) is particularly close to the transformation deceptions played on Maco. Finally, the device by which Rosso cheats Faccenda, the fishmonger, out of the eels so closely resembles Bibbiena's anecdote about the student who tricked a peasant out of a brace of capons (II, 88) that it may be a direct adaptation. Effectively, Aretino takes the native element of the practical joke from its literary foundations in the narratives of Boccaccio through the analysis of types and examples in Castiglione, who particularly attaches the *beffa* to the court milieu. He then blends it with the realistic mode of Roman New Comedy to create a plot vehicle "of dramatic contest or confrontation provided by the *beffa*, or practical joke."[40] The resulting comedic structure implicitly acknowledges and compliments its literary forebears, Bibbiena not least; at the same time it is a *paragone*, a competition, in which, again implicitly, Aretino outdoes these founding fathers.

Pasquino

Practical jokes are not a benign form of humor; the *beffa* is an aggressive assault on an individual, isolating him from the community and exposing him to ridicule, often entailing a loss of status or public image. In this respect the sequence of *beffe* might be seen as the plot equivalents of the equally aggressive verse satires called pasquinades (*pasquinate*). Richard Andrews, in fact, has drawn just this comparison, asserting, "The action of the play is (to use a modern analogy) animated cartoon farce, given significance by what amounts to a running commentary of *pasquinate* spoken in prose."[41]

"Pasquino" was the name given to a battered and broken classical statue that surfaced toward the end of the Quattrocento.[42] The statue was in such ruinous condition that almost a century passed

---

[40] Quotation from Andrews, *Scripts and Scenarios*, 67. On the Boccaccian origins of the dramatic *beffa*, see Jackson I. Cope, *Secret Sharers in Italian Comedy: From Machiavelli to Goldoni* (Durham, N.C.: Duke University Press, 1996), 18–19.

[41] Andrews, "Rhetoric and Drama," 164.

[42] The most useful account of Pasquino in English is a series of articles by Anne Reynolds on which I here rely. See "Cardinal Oliviero Carafa and the early Cinquecento Tradition of the Feast of Pasquino," *Humanistica Lovaniensia* 34A (1985): 178–208; "The Classical Continuum in Roman Humanism: The Festival of Pasquino, the Robigalia, and Satire," *Bibliothèque d'Humanisme et Renaissance* 49 (1987): 289–307; and "Classical Iconography in the Early Celebrations of the Festival of Pasquino," *Parergon* n.s. 5 (1987): 117–26.

before the figures represented were identified correctly as two Greek heroes from the Trojan War—Menelaus standing over the body of Patroclus. The humanist cardinal Oliviero Carafa obtained possession of the statue and in 1501 installed it on a pedestal before the Orsini palazzo, near the Piazza Navona. There it became one of the tourist sights of the city, as it is now. The custom of treating the mutilated statue as a kind of public notice-board by attaching anonymous Latin poems to it was established quite early, probably before it came under Carafa's sponsorship. In the same year that Carafa erected the statue, there is a record of satiric verses attacking the pope being attached to it. Although such verses could appear, as with our contemporary graffiti artists, whenever the impulse to satirize struck, the most notable event of the year was the Feast of Saint Mark on 25 April. On this occasion Pasquino was dressed in the costume of a god or other figure from Roman mythology and virtually buried in poems written on the specified theme. In 1509, the year of Janus, an enterprising printer began collecting these pasquinades and publishing the best of them in an annual volume. At first these poems were predominantly Latin, but a parallel volume of vernacular verse was printed in 1513, indicating the direction in which the poetic activity would go.

We cannot say with certainty just when Aretino entered the game of pasquinades, but it seems probable that he began writing them soon after his arrival in the city. He achieved public notoriety when, after the death of Leo X in 1520, he politicized the medium to an unusual degree during the 1521–22 conclave to elect a new pope. Aretino conducted a vociferous campaign to elect his own patron, Cardinal Giulio de' Medici, by slanderously discrediting the other candidates. Whereas the earlier humanist tradition had called for anonymous Latin verse, Aretino was pleased to insinuate his name into his Italian verses, and rival poets were quick to name him as a satiric target. This only had the effect of making him better known and causing an extraordinary number of pasquinades to be attributed to him. Despite Aretino's best efforts, Giulio lost the election and his poet prudently left the city. But Giulio did emerge the winner of the 1523 conclave, and Aretino was back in favor. Too much of a gadfly to enjoy it for long, however, Aretino offended Gian Matteo Giberti by his involvement in the 1524 *Modi* affair. Giberti was further exasperated by Aretino's behavior at the time of the 1525 Pasquino celebration. Although Giberti actively censored the printed volume, he could not control the public display of vituperative poems. The statue was dressed as Fortune, but Aretino boasted in a letter that Pasquino was celebrated in his name this year and, thereby, made fortunate ("A mio nome, questo anno se fa M. Pasquino, et fassi una fortuna"). Goaded beyond endurance, Giberti ordered the July assassination attempt that left Aretino with five knife wounds. After he was safely resident in Venice, Aretino continued to relish his identification with the genius of satire; two decades later he still referred to himself as Pasquino.

La cortigiana was written, and presumably circulated in manuscript, in the season of the 1525 Pasquino activities. Not surprisingly, the comedy is virtually a tribute to the spirit of Pasquino. Maestro Andrea, Maco's self-appointed tutor in courtiership and architect of the most outrageous practical jokes, was a real person — an artist, friend of Aretino, and composer of pasquinades, who later was killed during the Sack of Rome.[43] Andrea identifies Pasquino as a sharp-tongued poet "who plays filthy songs on his rebec," but tells his hapless pupil that it's not easy to learn who Pasquino really is (I, xxiv). Rosso compares himself to Marforio, Pasquino's counterpart (II, xviii); Valerio and Flaminio discuss the vicissitudes of Fortune (III, vii), and Rosso tries to persuade Parabolano that there are greater delights in life than women: "What about the honey that drops from tongues that can speak both the good and the evil?" Praise and blame were the objectives of demonstrative oratory, at this time a mode of speech

---

[43] Maestro Andrea is mentioned as a sculptor at the court of Leo X in Vasari's Life of Baccio Bandinelli. His name is linked with Aretino's in the "Confessione di Mastro Pasquino a Fra Mariano"; he is described as a painter in "Trionfo della lussuria di Maestro Pasquino." For these, see *Pasquino e dintorni: Testi pasquineschi del Cinquecento*, ed. Antonio Marzo (Rome: Salerno, 1990), 36, 106–08, 112. In Aretino's *Ragionamenti*, Nanna describes the trick that she played on an abusive lover with the aid of Maestro Andrea, who painted her face to look as if she had received a life-threatening wound. See Aretino's *Dialogues*, 204–06. In a letter of 15 May 1527, a fellow artist, Sebastiano del Piombo, informed Aretino of his friend's death.

particularly associated with preaching in the Roman curia.[44] But Rosso specifies that he means something superior to the sermons, verse satire: "Oh, those verses that Master Pasquino writes — they're marvellous! The barber says they should read one every day between the epistle and the gospel" (III, viii).

These internal references to Pasquino and pasquinades, of course, are set off by the Prologue with its genealogy of Pasquino and its praise of his dialogic versatility with language. The Prologue, it has been argued, implicitly but unmistakably attributes authorship of the comedy to Pasquino;[45] the extended implication would be that Histrion I is the voice of Aretino himself. The identification between Aretino and Pasquino serves several purposes: it distances the bite of the satire — Pasquino, after all, is a public institution and a civic ritual — while it exploits Aretino's current notoriety. At the same time, it provides a coherent perspective for both the broad physical comedy and the satiric set speeches.

Holding the Mirror up to Nature

In Act II, scene v, Sempronio, an old courtier, seeks Flaminio's advice on whether to place his son in service at the court. Times have changed, Flaminio replies. In Leo's day, a courtier would be amply rewarded — fed, clothed, provided with a horse and servant, and incidental expenses paid — but now the recompense is miserly, with the money instead going for "whores and boys." The abusive treatment of servants later receives confirmation in Rosso's vivid account of the repulsive meals provided in the *tinello*, the servants' dining hall (V, xiv). Whereas in Sempronio's recollection, "We were a band of brothers, each of us rich and each one a favorite," the present abuse of courtiers has the effect of corrupting them: "he'll become an envious, ambitious, wretched, ungrateful flatterer, a wicked, unjust, heretical hypocrite, a thief, an insolent lying glutton." Repeatedly the court is characterized by its

---

[44]See John W. O'Malley, *Praise and Blame in Renaissance Rome* (Durham, N.C.: Duke University Press, 1979).

[45]See Nino Borsellino, "La memoria teatrale di Pietro Aretino: i prologhi della *Cortigiana*," in *Il teatro italiano del Rinascimento*, ed. Lorch, 225–40.

irreligion (I, xxiv), dishonesty and enviousness (III, vii), cultivation of vices (V, vii), and pervasive homosexuality (III, vi).

A particular refrain asserts the blind arbitrariness with which masters, whether nobles or churchmen, advance favorites. Valerio, the honest courtier whose name labels his character, comments bitterly that a Rosso will become "a big man at court" before any scholar (I, xii), and complains that "You nobles . . . control fortune! You raise up vice and ignorance from the stables, and then down into the stables you throw virtue" (I, xxii). The plot proves his accusation, as Parabolano discharges Valerio while advancing Rosso. Even though Valerio regains his position and receives an apology in the end, he does not change his belief: "all they do is spoil good men, and ruin them forever" (V, xxi). Master Andrea believes that office-holders are the very worst of all, driven mad by power and vanity (I, xxiii). The theme of blind fortune may well have been chosen to make the comedy suitable for performance during the Feast of Pasquino. Aretino's analysis of the sickness pervading the Roman court, however, is most interesting in its "trickle-down" thesis: the rot at the top infects the courtiers, who in turn affect household servants like Rosso, who take out their own frustrations and hostility not only on their betters but on ordinary people. Rosso spitefully betrays both Parabolano and Valerio, but warms up with such lesser game as the Jewish peddler and the fishmonger, who delivers the appropriate malediction: "Damn Rome, the court, the church, everyone who lives here, and everyone who believes in it!" (I, xxi). Rosso, after causing Romanello to be jailed, agrees: "Oh, the crooked things that go on here in this filthy Rome of ours! God must be truly patient, or he'd have sent down some great calamity by now" (IV, xvii). The fantasy fulfillment of the two plots empowers tricky servants; Master Andrea and Rosso lead their "betters" by their noses, exposing the ruling class as fools. At the same time, the logic of the argument makes the absence of punishments in the denouement something more than the usual comedic reconciliation or renewal of society: because those in power have motivated the behavior of their servants, they alone are guilty.

The Roman society that Aretino so vividly recreates actually is a cleverly contrived palimpsest, superimposing Leonine Rome upon Clementine. Angelo Romano has insisted that we cannot fully understand the *Cortigiana* if we do not recognize how completely it is saturated in the atmosphere of Leo's court.[46] Although the time of the action ostensibly is contemporary, 1525, the great majority of references to events and individuals, as the notes indicate, evoke a past time, the Golden Age of Leo's reign and Sempronio's nostalgia. Even Maco's naïve assumption that he can become a cardinal serves as a veiled reminder of the wholesale elevations by Leo. This double perspective has the effect of displacing and distancing social criticism, so that responsibility does not attach to Clement. The pope is praised both indirectly through his officials (IV, xiv and V, vii) and directly. Flaminio, the other good courtier, believes that "justice needs the help of Pope Clement" (III, xii) and plans to go to Mantua until Clement sorts out the world: "His Holiness will put virtue back where it belongs, just as his brother Leo did" (III, vii). As a satirist who yet is an aspiring courtier, Aretino must walk a fine line. His own merit has not been appropriately recognized and rewarded, he believes; but, to keep the possibility of advancement alive, he needs to avoid completely alienating Clement and his advisors, while nonetheless advertising the power of his pen. The tactic that he adopts, representing conditions that came to flourish under Leo and, while not disparaging Leo, urging Clement to correct them, itself might be taken from the armory of the *Cortegiano*. For Castiglione, the courtier's highest purpose is to serve his prince by advising him "in a gentle manner" to avoid a wrong course of action, which requires "know[ing] how to find means timely and fitting to attain that good end" (IV, 5). Were Castiglione still in Rome, he surely would have admired the deftness with which his precept had been adapted to another medium.

The outrageous image of Maco in the courtier mold offers one thematic center for the play; another, perhaps equally rich, comes

---

[46]See Angelo Romano, "Appunti sui personaggi della *Cortigiana* (1525) dell' Aretino," in *Scenery, Set, and Staging in the Italian Renaissance*, 121–36 (with English summary). He discusses eleven characters or names taken from real life. Aside from Master Andrea, these are: Grillo, Cosimo Baraballo, Accursio and Serpica, Mariano Fetti, Rosso, Domenico Brandino, Giovan Battista de' Nobili, Mario Bracci, and Bartolomeo Pattolo. If one included the obvious names—Giberti, Clement, Leo himself—the count would go up.

with Master Andrea's concave mirror. Poor Maco has been boiled like a lobster in hot water, purged by the emetic medlars, shaved, and dressed in new clothes (IV, xiii), and he demands, "Show me the mirror. I feel like a new man!" (IV, xviii). Seeing his distorted features, Maco throws himself on the ground, crying that he is mutilated, ruined, dead, changed in form by visible and invisible thieves. In short, "Io non son io!" ('I am not I'). Andrea, substituting a plain mirror, persuades Maco to look again, and he is jubilant — put right again and handsomer than ever — ready to be not merely a courtier but pope. One needs to reflect that Maco, the most memorably bumptious character in the comedy, has an endearing awareness of just how tenuous is his identity. Without Sanese and Andrea, he is lost; disguised as a porter, he plaintively asks Andrea to "walk close behind; someone might steal me from myself" (II, xxiii). With Grillo dressed in his clothes, and persuaded that the police are looking for "Maco," he becomes thoroughly muddled about his own identity. By chance encountering Parabolano, who inquires, "You are Messer Maco?" he replies gratefully, "Yes, I am, I am!" Aretino plays astutely with the sense of anonymity, even anomie that emerges from the Pandora's box of urban life. The frangibility of social identity is underscored by costume change — Romanello the Jew beaten by the outraged officer for wearing a friar's robe, Togna prudently wearing her husband's clothing to avoid possible gang-rape, Ercolano forced to venture out in Togna's clothes — but nowhere more poignantly than with Maco, his new courtier's finery gone and demonstrating to the world that "the traitors made a hole in my ass with their swords!"

Master Andrea's use of a concave mirror smacks of an in-joke from Roman artistic circles. The previous year, the handsome and precocious young artist Parmigianino had arrived in Rome bearing three samples of his work, and gained an audience with the pope. Clement was charmed by the artist, and suitably impressed by the work, of which one example was the *Self-Portrait in a Convex Mirror*. The pictorial surface creates the illusion of the mirror in which we see the artist's reflection; its convexity causes the distortion of the artist's enlarged right hand in the lower foreground. An obvious, if literal-minded, reading of the portrait might be that the elegantly dressed young man presents his hand in service to a prospective patron. Clement VII apparently obtained the painting, whether by gift or purchase, and later presented it to Aretino. If Vasari's somewhat muddled account can be relied upon, the *Self-Portrait* must have come into Aretino's possession in late 1524 or early 1525, certainly before he abandoned Rome after the assassination attempt. One can appreciate, then, why he had portraits in distorting mirrors on his mind at the time he was writing *La cortigiana*. As Jodi Cranston has remarked, the mirror serves as a metaphor of "Maco's folly and misguided self-perception."[47] Maco accepts the first mirror image as "true," believing that the distorted image accurately shows how his identity has melted in the courtier mold; then, seeing himself in the plain mirror, he accepts that he is not only restored, but transformed into a perfect courtier. The image that he now accepts as "true" is even more a distortion of reality than that in the concave mirror.

The implied comment on Maco's folly is the most immediate function of the mirror image, but not the only one. During the sixteenth century the concept of imitation was foundational in both rhetoric and poetics. Rhetorical "imitation" largely meant the imitation of classical models, as, for example, the *commedia erudita* "imitated" the forms and rules discerned in Plautus and Terence. In poetic theory, largely under the dominance of Aristotle, it was accepted that literature is an imitation or representation (*mimesis*) of human actions. Donatus attributes to Cicero the definition that comedy is "an imitation of life, a mirror of custom, an image of truth," thereby spawning an endless succession of mirror metaphors in Renaissance literary theory.[48] The most familiar of these, Hamlet's advice to the players, has behind it the force of an entire century: "the purpose of playing . . . both at the first and now, was and is, to hold as 'twere the mirror up to nature, to show virtue her feature, scorn her own image, and the very

---

[47] Jodi Cranston, *The Poetics of Portraiture in the Italian Renaissance* (Cambridge: Cambridge University Press, 2000), 151; and see 140–50 on Parmigianino's *Self-Portrait*. She reviews Vasari's comments (142–43) but does not notice that the dates render his claim to have seen the portrait in Aretino's house in Arezzo "as a young boy" impossible.

[48] Quoted from Baxter Hathaway, *The Age of Criticism: The Late Renaissance in Italy* (Ithaca: Cornell University Press, 1962), 5.

age and body of the time his form and pressure" (III, ii, 20–24).[49] Showing "virtue her feature, scorn her own image" places Hamlet's concept of theater in the province of demonstrative rhetoric, a mode with which Aretino must have become familiar, in a fine irony, from the current style of sermon oratory in Rome. In a larger sense, Andrea's mirror is a metonym for the action of the comedy itself, in which Aretino holds up a mirror to the very age and body of the time. For one critic, "the portrait of the city of Rome" is the "only nucleus" of the play.[50] The reflected image of themselves that the audience should see, of course, is not that of a new Golden Age Rome, but, rather, the courtesan Rome, a city in which anything and everything can be bought. As Rosso says admiringly to Aloigia, "You've got Rome under your thumb!" (II, vi).

Finally, it has been observed, "The Renaissance Aristotelian usually interpreted the poet's imitation as the making of a portrait of a real-life subject."[51] Conversant with the visual arts to the extent that he thought of himself as a fellow artist, Aretino surely knew the aphorism that "every painter paints himself" ("Ogni dipintore dipinge sè"). Beyond Parabolano's admiring account of the *beffa* executed by "Pietro Aretino" (V, xvi), various characters within the comedy have been identified with Aretino himself. In the Prologue, Histrion I, as has been mentioned, is associated with Pasquino, Aretino's alter ego in the mid-twenties. Within the play itself, the two masters of ceremonies carry the same associations. Both Andrea and Rosso talk about Pasquino; Rosso compares himself to Marforio, the statue of a river god that carried on satiric dialogues with Pasquino—a dynamic that underscores the similarity of their roles in the two plots. With Andrea—artist, writer of pasquinades, and real-life friend—the relation to Aretino is particularly insistent; equally, however, Rosso's set speech on the

---

[49] Quoted from *The Riverside Shakespeare*, gen. ed. G.B. Evans, 2nd ed. (Boston: Houghton Mifflin, 1997).

[50] See Radcliff-Umstead, *The Birth of Modern Comedy*, 165.

[51] Baxter Hathaway, *Marvels and Commonplaces: Renaissance Literary Criticism*, Studies in Language and Literature (New York: Random House, 1968), 44. See further Marc Bizer, "The Reflection of the Other in One's Own Mirror: The Idea of the Portrait in Renaissance Imitatio," *Romance Notes* 36 (1996): 191–99.

disgusting meals provided for servants, which has no plot function, has been taken as Aretino's own bitterly-felt experience. The disenchanted courtier Flaminio plans to leave Rome for Mantua and the protection of Frederigo Gonzaga, as Aretino had done after the election of Adrian VI and as he would do again in 1526; yet Flaminio also voices the praise of Clement, seemingly aimed at getting Aretino the desired preferment. The multiple avatars of the playwright reinforce the thesis of Giulio Ferroni that the effect of Aretino's words is to overpower the fictive characters and action, causing the audience to relate more immediately to the author.[52] Whereas his Paduan contemporary Ruzzante (Angelo Beolco) achieved a similar effect by both writing and acting in his plays, Aretino does it with words alone. In the multiple reflections of the mirror that is *La cortigiana*, the audience sees themselves, Rome, and, not least, a portrait of Pietro Aretino.

---

[52]See Giulio Ferroni, *Le voci dell' istrione: Pietro Aretino e la dissoluzione del teatro* (Naples: Liguori, 1977).

Select Bibliography

Primary Sources

Aretino, Pietro. *Aretino's Dialogues*. Trans. Raymond Rosenthal, 1971. Reprint with Epilogue by Margaret F. Rosenthal. New York: Marsilio, 1994.

——. *Aretino: Selected Letters*. Trans. George Bull. Harmondsworth: Penguin, 1976.

——. *La Cortigiana*. Ed. Giuliano Innamorati. Collezione di teatro 137, 1970. Reprint, Turin: Einaudi, 1980.

——. *Edizione nazionale delle opere di Pietro Aretino*. Ed. Giovanni Aquilecchia and Angelo Romano. Rome: Salerno, 1992– .

——. *The Marescalco*. Trans. J. Douglas Campbell and Leonard G. Sbrocchi. Carleton Renaissance Plays in Translation 10. 2nd ed. Ottawa: Dovehouse Editions, 1992. [1986]

——. (with Giulio Romano, Marcantonio Raimondi, Count Jean-Frederic-Maximilien De Waldeck). *I Modi: The Sixteen Pleasures, An Erotic Album of the Italian Renaissance*. Ed. and trans. Lynne Lawner. Evanston, Ill.: Northwestern University Press, 1988. Includes verse trans. of the *Sonetti lussuriosi*.

——. *Tutte le opere di Pietro Aretino*. Vol. 2: *Teatro*. Ed. Giorgio Petrocchi. Milan: Mondadori, 1971.

Ariosto, Lodovico. *The Comedies of Ariosto*. Ed. and trans. Edmund M. Beame and Leonard G. Sbrocchi. Chicago: University of Chicago Press, 1975.

Bembo, Pietro. *Prose e rime*. Ed. Carlo Dionisotti. Classici italiani 26. 2nd ed. Turin: Unione Tipografico-Editrice Torinese, 1966. [1960]

Bruno, Giordano. *Candlebearer*. Trans. Gino Moliterno. Ottawa: Dovehouse Editions, 2000.

Castiglione, Baldasare. *The Book of the Courtier*. Trans. Charles S. Singleton. Anchor Books. Garden City, N.Y.: Doubleday, 1959.

Delicado, Francisco. *Portrait of Lozana, The Lusty Andalusian Woman*. Trans. Bruno M. Damiani. Scripta Humanistica 34. Potomac, Md., 1987.

Dovizi da Bibbiena, Bernardo. *The Follies of Calandro*. Trans. Oliver Evans. In *The Genius of the Italian Theater*. Ed. Eric Bentley. New York: New American Library, 1964, 31–98. [Includes Castiglione's Prologue and letter describing the 1513 performance, 511–15.]

Florio, John. *A Worlde of Wordes, or most copious, and exact dictionarie in Italian and English*. London, 1598. Facsimile ed. Hildesheim: Georg Olms, 1972.

Guicciardini, Francesco. *The History of Italy*. Ed. and trans. Sidney Alexander, 1969. Reprint, Princeton: Princeton University Press, 1984.

Machiavelli, Niccolo. *The Comedies of Machiavelli*. Ed. and trans. David Sices and James B. Atkinson. Hanover, N.H.: University Press of New England, 1985.

Pasquino e dintorni: Testi pasquineschi del Cinquecento. Ed. Antonio Marzo. Rome: Salerno, 1990.

Shakespeare, William. *The Riverside Shakespeare*. Gen. ed. G.B. Evans. 2nd ed. Boston: Houghton Mifflin, 1997.

Vasari, Giorgio. *Lives of the Painters, Sculptors, and Architects*. Trans. Gaston du C. de Vere. Intro. David Ekserdjian. 2 vols. New York: Knopf, 1996.

Secondary Studies

Andrews, Richard. "Rhetoric and Drama: Monologues and Set Speeches in Aretino's Comedies." *The Languages of Literature in Renaissance Italy*, ed. Peter Hainsworth et al. Oxford: Clarendon, 1988. 153–68.

———. *Scripts and Scenarios: The Performance of Comedy in Renaissance Italy*. Cambridge: Cambridge University Press, 1993.

Barish, Jonas. "The Problem of Closet Drama in the Italian Renaissance." *Italica* 71 (1994): 4–30.

Bizer, Marc. "The Reflection of the Other in One's Own Mirror: The Idea of the Portrait in Renaissance Imitatio." *Romance Notes* 36 (1996): 191–99.

Boggione, Valter, and Giovanni Casalegno. *Dizionario storico del lessico erotico italiano*. Milan: Longanei, 1996.

Cairns, Christopher. *Pietro Aretino and the Republic of Venice: Researches on Aretino and His Circle in Venice, 1527–1556*. Biblioteca dell' "Archivium Romanicum" 194. Florence: Olschki, 1985.

———, ed. *Scenery, Set and Staging in the Italian Renaissance: Studies in the Practice of Theatre*. Lewiston, N.Y.: Edwin Mellen, 1996.

Chastel, André. *The Sack of Rome, 1527*. Trans. Beth Archer. Bollingen Series 35. Princeton: Princeton University Press, 1983.

Cope, Jackson I. *Secret Sharers in Italian Comedy: From Machiavelli to Goldoni*. Durham, N.C.: Duke University Press, 1996.

Cranston, Jodi. *The Poetics of Portraiture in the Italian Renaissance*. Cambridge: Cambridge University Press, 2000.

Damiani, Bruno M. *Francisco Delicado*. Twaynes World Authors Series 335. New York: Twayne, 1974.

Dandelet, Thomas James. *Spanish Rome: 1500–1700*. New Haven: Yale University Press, 2001.

Ferroni, Giulio. *Le voci dell' istrione: Pietro Aretino e la dissoluzione del teatro*. Naples: Liguori, 1977.

Firpo, Massimo. *Il Sacco di Roma del 1527: Tra profezia, propaganda politica e riforma religiosa*. Cagliari, 1990.

Günsberg, Maggie. *Gender and the Italian Stage: From the Renaissance to the Present Day*. Cambridge: Cambridge University Press, 1997.

Hathaway, Baxter. *The Age of Criticism: The Late Renaissance in Italy*. Ithaca, N.Y.: Cornell University Press, 1962.

———. *Marvels and Commonplaces: Renaissance Literary Criticism*. Studies in Language and Literature. New York: Random House, 1968.

Herrick, Marvin T. *Italian Comedy in the Renaissance*. Urbana: University of Illinois Press, 1960.

Imperiale, Louis. *La Roma clandestina de Francisco Delicado y Pietro Aretino*. Studies on Cervantes and His Times 6. New York: Peter Lang, 1997.

Larivaille, Paul. *Pietro Aretino fra Rinascimento e manierismo*. Rome: Bolzoni, 1980.

Lawner, Lynne. *Lives of the Courtesans: Portraits of the Renaissance*. New York: Rizzoli, 1987.

Lorch, Maristella de Panizza, ed. *Il teatro italiano del Rinascimento*. Saggi di cultura contemporanea 134. Milan: Edizione di Comunità, 1980.

Melchiori, Angiolina. "Emblems of Renaissance Theatre: A Study of Aretino's Comedies." Ph.D. diss., Yale University, 1988.

Mitchell, Bonner. *Rome in the High Renaissance: The Age of Leo X*. Norman: University of Oklahoma Press, 1973.

O'Malley, John W. *Praise and Blame in Renaissance Rome*. Durham, N.C.: Duke University Press, 1979.

Palladino, Lora Anne. "Pietro Aretino: Orator and Art Theorist." Ph.D. diss., Yale University, 1981.

Partner, Peter. *Renaissance Rome 1500–1559: A Portrait of a Society*. Berkeley and Los Angeles: University of California Press, 1976

Partridge, Loren. *The Renaissance in Rome, 1400–1600*. Everyman Art Library. London: George Weidenfeld and Nicolson, 1996.

Pietro Aretino nel cinquecentenario della nascita. 2 vols. Pubblicazioni del Centro Pio Rajna, ser. 1, no. 4. Rome: Salerno, 1995.

Quondam, Amedeo. "La scena della menzogna: Corte e cortigiano nel 'Ragionamento' di Pietro Aretino." *Psicon*, nos. 8–9 (1978): 4–23.

Radcliff-Umstead, Douglas. *The Birth of Modern Comedy in Renaissance Italy*. Chicago: University of Chicago Press, 1969.

Reynolds, Anne. "Cardinal Oliviero Carafa and the early Cinquecento Tradition of the Feast of Pasquino." *Humanistica Lovaniensia* 34A (1985): 178–208.

———. "The Classical Continuum in Roman Humanism: The Festival of Pasquino, the Robigalia, and Satire." *Bibliothèque d'Humanisme et Renaissance* 49 (1987): 289–307.

———. "Classical Iconography in the Early Celebration of the Festival of Pasquino." *Parergon*, n.s. 5 (1987): 117–26.

———, ed. and trans. *Renaissance Humanism at the Court of Clement VII: Francesco Berni's Dialogue Against Poets in Context*. Garland Studies in the Renaissance 7. New York: Garland, 1997.

Rosenthal, Margaret F. *The Honest Courtesan: Veronica Franco, Citizen and Writer in Sixteenth-Century Venice*. Chicago: University of Chicago Press, 1992.

Rowland, Ingrid D. *The Culture of the High Renaissance: Ancients and Moderns in Sixteenth-Century Rome*. Cambridge: Cambridge University Press, 1998.

Ruggiero, Guido. *Binding Passions: Tales of Magic, Marriage, and Power and the End of the Renaissance*. New York: Oxford University Press, 1993.

Stinger, Charles L. *The Renaissance in Rome*. Bloomington: Indiana University Press, 1985.

Stollhans, Cynthia. "Fra Mariano, Peruzzi and Polidoro da Caravaggio: A New Look at Religious Landscapes in Renaissance Rome." *Sixteenth Century Journal* 23 (1992): 506–25.

Talvacchia, Bette. *Taking Positions: On the Erotic in Renaissance Culture*. Princeton: Princeton University Press, 1999. [Includes prose trans. of Aretino's *Sonetti lussuriosi*.]

Ulysse, Georges. "La Cruauté comme révélateur: L'example de la *Cortigiana* de l'Aretin." *Cahiers d'Études Romanes* 18 (1994): 175–86.

Cortigiana

[1525]

Dramatis Personae

HISTRION I
HISTRION II

MESSER MACO, a young gentleman from Siena
SANESE, servant to MESSER MACO
GRILLO, servant to MESSER MACO

PARABOLANO, a Roman gentleman
VALERIO, steward to PARABOLANO
FLAMINIO, a courtier in service to PARABOLANO
ROSSO, servant to PARABOLANO
CAPPA, servant to PARABOLANO

SEMPRONIO, an elderly former courtier

MASTER ANDREA
ZOPPINO, a pimp
MASTER MERCURIO, a doctor
ALOIGIA, a bawd

TOGNA, wife of ERCOLANO
ERCOLANO, a baker

A SELLER OF BOOKS AND PAPERS
A FISHMONGER
A SACRISTAN
PRIESTS
FATHER GUARDIAN OF ARACELI
ROMANELLO, a Jewish merchant
A POLICEMAN

BIASINA, maid to CAMILLA PISANA

La Cortigiana

Prologue

HISTRION I: I had learned a kind of prologue—a piece of nonsense, part gossip, part double-talk, part plot summary—call it an introduction if you like. I was going to perform it for you for the sake of a friend of mine, but everyone wants to make trouble for me. Look—if you know what's good for you, you'll just applaud and go home.

HISTRION II: What? Applaud and go home? After all the work I've done on this... this abstract, this argument—whatever the hell you want to call it—trying to make this shit flow smoothly? And now you want me to throw it away? You're about as straight as the Tower of Pisa! And the way you throw your weight around!

HISTRION I: O.K., O.K. So I made a mistake. No need to crucify me! It's only a play!

HISTRION II: Yeah, you're right. It wouldn't be fair or proper to crucify a person over something as trivial as that.

HISTRION I: They crucify people for nothing at all. You want proof? A Roman named Messer Mario[1] who came to see me a while back wants to get me in hot water for calling him a pimp.

HISTRION II: Ha, ha, ha!

HISTRION I: Go ahead, have a good laugh, but I feel more like crying. As soon as this Mario guy left, Ceccotto the Genoese,[2] who used to be a tailor but who's into astrology now, jumped on me, accusing me of saying that Spaniards are better than Frenchmen. And even that fool Lorenzo Luti[3] almost drew a knife on me, saying I'd bad-mouthed him and called him a fool just because he's from Siena. And that Lady Maggiorina,[4] the Roman sawbones, is screaming her head off because someone told her I think she's a witch. There's a thousand stories like that. I don't want my boss to think I'm that kind of person. It's important what kind of impression you make, especially on the big shots.

HISTRION II: You might as well just lie down and die if you're going to worry about what impression you're making on the big shots. You worry too much about offending them. Their good will's worth about as much to you as the jubilee[5] was to Girolamo Beltramo.[6] Now let's get serious: give us your damned prologue, I'll give these gentlemen a dose of plot summary, and then whoever's going to play the comedy, let them get on with it! As for me, once I've done my job, that's that. I've got the plot summary right here.

HISTRION I: Now I hope you're all happy, and anyone who takes offence can just scratch his ass.

You can look wherever you want[7] — not just in Italy but the whole world — and you'll never find another crowd of loafers like this, all gathered in one place. You all rushed in when you heard the racket, but none of you had any idea what it was all about. At least when they had that doctor from Vercelli[8] and his friends drawn and quartered, people knew the whys and wherefores of it a couple of days beforehand. Now I suppose some wise guy out there's going to say he just came to enjoy the show — as if a play has nothing else to do but make him laugh. You won't shut up, eh? I'm warning you — I wouldn't hesitate to expose every last one of you. By God, if you don't shut up I'll sic the dog on you. I'll tell everyone which of you are doing it, and which of you are having it done.[9] If it weren't for the respect I have for Milady Comedia, who'd find herself deserted, I'd make all your sins a matter of public record. I know all about them — better than the Marches know the kind and saintly memory of Armelino[10] (if you'll pardon my mentioning it).

Some of you should be out paying rent for your lady's house, or seeing that her servant gets his salary.

If there's anyone here who's had a falling out with the steward, you should be trying to set things straight with him. And if there's anyone who hasn't eaten, please go in now, before the bells ring to announce that it's time for supper. And if you haven't said your offices yet, I'm sure it wouldn't be a sin against the Holy Ghost if you didn't say them now.

Now if you're a father or a brother with a son or brother at court, and you're putting up with all kinds of hardships to keep him there, to make a Messer or a Reverend out of him, you can congratulate yourself, because the great benefit he'll end up with is that he'll be able to chase after fairy tales.

But I'm wasting my breath; and anyway I can see that you'd rather I told you about the play. Come on, loafers, pay attention! Are you going to sit down or aren't you? Some of you are sitting on very uncomfortable seats. Why? To watch a story. If you felt as uncomfortable as that at St. Peter's, when it came time to view the Blessed Countenance[11] you'd tell Messer Lord God you're coming back to see him some other time. You know, you're lucky there are some honest women (well, a few, anyway), because you'll find yourself in hot water, and it won't be orange water, I'll tell you that! But let's get back to business.

Milords, you're my patrons, and, although you may think I sometimes go a little too far, you've got nothing to be afraid of. You're all noble, decent, and courteous men, and you can take a joke. Don't think that you're going to dislike this bit of nonsense we're about to show you — it was written with you in mind.

It makes me laugh to think about it: before the curtain opened, you probably thought it was the Tower of Babel back there, but instead it was Rome itself. Look: there's the Palace, St. Peter's, the piazza, the fortress, a couple of taverns — the Hare and the Luna — the fountain, St. Catherine's — the whole thing.[12]

There: now that you can see that it's Rome (you can see the Colosseum and the Pantheon, all sorts of things), and there's no doubt that it'll be a comedy, what do you think it's called? *The Courtesan.* Her father's from Tuscany and her mother's from Bergamo,[13] but don't be surprised if she dispenses with those melt-in-your-mouth sonnets, with their Oils, and their Crystalline Liquids, and their Nevermores, their Hithers and

Thithers, or any of that kind of crap, because Miladies the Muses eat nothing but delicate little Florentine salads.¹⁴ I'll have you know that I'm a follower of the Bolognese cavalier, Cassio de' Medici,¹⁵ a poet, so it seems, who in one of his works on the lives of the saints writes this divine and memorable verse:

Per noi fe' Cristo in su la croce el tomo.*

Now you'd never catch Petrarch using *tomo* for "fool" — it was that pompous ass from Bologna (and he was no Petrarch).¹⁶ Just like Cinotto,¹⁷ another Bolognese patrician, when he wrote against the Turk:

Fa che tu sippa, Padre santo, in mare,
El Turco deroccando e tartussando
Che Dio si vuol con tecco scorrucciare.†

Sippa is an archaic word; *deroccare* and *tartussare* are modern. Cinotto was crowned as a poet by Pope Leo,¹⁸ so I suppose it's all right for him to use them, but there are commentators on Petrarch's vocabulary who make him say things that even Nocca da Firenze,¹⁹ who kept his silence after they tortured him in his hometown, wouldn't have said even if you were to torture him some more.²⁰

No one knows better than Pasquino²¹ what words can or can't be used. He has a book that traces his genealogy, and you can read many fine things there, as you'll hear, because although he's the son of a poet, here I make him a writer of prose. Parnassus²² is such a high, rugged devil of a mountain that Saint Francis himself²³ wouldn't climb it, not even to receive the stigmata. That place belonged to a poor gentleman by the name of Apollo, who — either out of desperation or because of some vow — built a hermitage and lived there. Now it happened that someone — I don't know who — touched the hearts of nine fine ladies. These ladies, having been received

---

*'For us Christ, on the cross, played the fool.'

†'Holy Father, the Turk is on the seas destroying and harassing — because God wants you to know that he is angry with you.'

by the aforementioned Apollo, entered the monastery with him and took their vows, and it wasn't long before they fell deeply in love with him.

Now since the devil happens to be subtle, Milord Apollo handsome, and Miladies the Muses very beautiful indeed, the marriage was consummated, and sons and daughters were born. And because Apollo was a good singer, as you can tell from his lyre and from the many years he sang and played in the public square, all his sons and daughters were poets. Now when it came to be known that on that mountain there were nine beautiful women all at the beck and call of one man, many people climbed to the top through hard work and talent, while many others, who thought they could make the climb, broke their necks instead. The moment the Muses, kind ladies that they were, saw that they could give Apollo a rest, they made those who had been clever enough to climb that devil of a mountain feel very much at home, with the result that they placed invisible horns on the head of that gentle creature Apollo. This was the alchemy that produced Pasquino, no one knows from which Muse or from which poet. He is a bastard, that's for certain. And anyone who says that these Muses are sisters is mistaken—he reads the chronicles about as accurately as Mainaldo the Mantuan[24] judges his antiques and his jewels. They're not even related! Look at how many languages there are to be read. Pasquino's a case in point: sometimes he speaks Greek, sometimes Corsican, or French, or German, Bergamese, Genoese, Venetian, Neapolitan. This is because one Muse was born in Bergamo, another in France, this one in the Romagna, that one in Chiasso—and then Calliope, of course, was born in Tuscany. You can imagine whether a mixture like that could produce sisters! The reason why Tuscan's more pleasing than the others is that when Petrarch was in Avignon, he fell in love with Laura, who was a servant of Calliope and spoke just like her. Now Francesco liked the sweet tongue of Milady Laura, and he began to write in praise of her, and, since no other style matches his—except perhaps that of the Abbot of Gaeta[25]—we must follow his authority. As far as the spoken word is concerned, you can do what you want, provided of course that you don't tell the truth. A Milanese, for instance, can say *micca* for "bread," and a Bolognese can say *sippa* for "he."

HISTRION II: My God! Now if you were reading the charge and sentence at the trial of a *podestà*,[26] that might sound great. It was quite a speech! What the hell do you care about these language questions? I thought you'd never finish. I'd have been here all day with this thing in my hand, and it'd get cold, and these people would get only half of the plot.

HISTRION I: You're right. But could you give me some inkling of what spices you've put in this plot summary[27] to ease the flow, because if you've used Slenders, and Tendrils, and Zephyrs, and Tranquils, and Serene Countenances, and Refulgent Rubies, and Silken Pearls, and Limpid Words, and Honeyed Glances, well, they're so dry and stiff that they'd stop up the bowels of an ostrich — and as you know, an ostrich can digest a nail.

HISTRION II: What did I put in it? Shit! That's what! Now shut up and wait until I've told the story — then you can talk to me.

HISTRION I: Go ahead then.

The Argument

HISTRION II: This'll be good for you, what I've got in here. The way it's put together, it could draw laughter from tears itself. Messer Maco De Coe from Siena, *studiante in libris*,* has come to Rome to put himself in the service of some pope, as a cardinal. Once, when he was almost dead with brain fever, his father swore that if the boy recovered, he, the elder Maco, would see that he became a cardinal in the service of a pope. His wish was granted. The son is now as healthy as ever, and a little handsomer, and his father, to fulfil the vow he made for his son's recovery, has sent him to Rome. Master Andrea, whom he takes as a teacher, makes him believe that you can't become a cardinal in the service of a pope just like that; first you've got to become a courtier. Andrea has no difficulty making him believe a story about a certain Gioan Manente de Reggio,[28] who went to a foundry to have himself made into a courtier. By means of this wonderful piece of nonsense he

---

*'A student of books.'

takes this ineffable fool to the public baths, where, he tells him, there are molds that make the most handsome courtiers in the world. So Messer Maco turns himself from an ass into an ox, and makes all the wise and witty words of crazy old Mastro Andrea[29] come true. You'd never believe a man could be so stupid, except that you can see even greater miracles than that at court any day of the week. Take the Elephant's Will.[30] Now that, it seems to me, was a much bigger thing, because the beast itself was so huge. Or hearing Master Pasquino, who's made of marble, talking sense. And you know, it still seems miraculous to me to see the likes of Accursio and Serapica ruling the world — one of them used to look after the farms of Caradoso the goldsmith, and the other was keeper of the kennels.[31] But that's enough moral philosophy for now.

Seven cities fought over Homer;[32] each one has always wanted to claim him as its own. That's not quite the way it happens with Messer Maco: more than thirty towns have declined to acknowledge him; no one wants him, either as a friend or a relative. Milan rejects him as a simpleton, Mantua as a fool, Venice as an asshole; even Matelica[33] rejects him. To settle the dispute we've brought the case to trial, and with the audience's co-operation it will, like many things, soon come to a conclusion. Today we'll make him a Sienese; tomorrow, whoever wants him can have him.

And we have something else I think you'll enjoy: Parabolano the Neapolitan, another Accursio, at court more through the whim of fortune than through his own merits, will fall in love. He's pining away for Laura, the wife of Sir Luzio, a Roman. He doesn't want anyone to know about this amour, but one of his rascally servants, hearing his master moaning about her in his sleep, discovers the secret. He makes his master believe that Laura is in love with him, and, with the help of a procuress, he manages to get them together. As a result, this big shot, dumb as they get, finds himself mixed up with a baker, who's fouler than villainy itself. What with all this happening, you'll witness a small sampling of the courtly ways of men and women, and you'll see two comedies born and die on the same stage. But don't be afraid, Milady Comedia Cortigiana is falser than the chimera, more unpleasant than trouble, truer than honesty, sweeter than harmony, jollier than happiness, more irritable than anger, sillier than buffoonery, and, to tell the truth, bolder than insolence. And if you see Messer Maco or the others coming on the scene more than six times, don't fret yourself — Rome is a free city, and the chains that hold the mills on the river couldn't hold back these crazy asses . . . I mean "actors." So don't get excited if somebody speaks out of character—this isn't Athens: they do things differently here. Besides, the fellow who wrote this story has a mind of his own, and the Bishop of Chieti himself[34] couldn't reform him.

HISTRION I: You really ladle it out by the bucketful, don't you (as Messer Zanozzo Pandolfini[35] used to say)! My God, you handle a plot summary like a master! It was like a good laxative! Now let's step aside and listen to what Messer Maco will do to become a courtier. There he is. Ha, ha, ha! Oh what a fool! Ha, ha, eh, ho!

Act I

[Scene i.]

(MESSER MACO, *the master, and* SANESE, *his servant*)

MESSER MACO: Well, Rome sure is the *capus mundi*.* And if I hadn't come here . . .

SANESE: The bread would be mouldy.

MESSER MACO: Holy shit! I never would've believed it! It's a thousand times prettier than Siena!

SANESE: I told you, didn't I? Rome's not only a little prettier than Siena, but a bit bigger too. But "No," you said, "in Siena we've got the academy, and all the scholars, and the Fonte Branda, and the Fonte Beccia; there's the piazza, and the palace[36] — and then in the middle of August we've got the running of the bulls, and the carts with all their candles and their waterworks, and a thousand other things. We make marzipan in Siena and *bericuocoli*† by the hundreds; the Emperor loves us, and just about everyone else does too — except the Florentines."

MESSER MACO: It was true what you told me: you never see men as well dressed as this in Siena, riding along on horseback with their servants. This is wonderful!

SANESE: Ssh! Listen! A woodpecker's talking.

MESSER MACO: A parrot, you mean, you damned fool!

SANESE: It's a woodpecker, not a parrot.

MESSER MACO: And I say a parrot, not a woodpecker!

SANESE: Sorry to say this, boss, but you're a fool. This is one of those an ancestor of yours bought for three lire and sent

---

*Head of the world

†A Sienese cookie made with flour and honey and garnished with pine nuts, pistachios, or ground almonds.

to Corsignano, only to find he'd sent the wrong one. Or so Morgante said.[37]

MESSER MACO: Morgante didn't like us, Sanese. When I showed one of the feathers to the brassworker, he said it was a parrot's, and a fine one at that.

SANESE: Boss, you don't know birds.

MESSER MACO: I do so, damn you!

SANESE: Don't get mad!

MESSER MACO: I'll get mad if I damned well please. I'd like some obedience and respect—and when I say something I expect to be believed.

SANESE: I respect you like a ducat, I obey you like a servant, and I believe you as if you were—Messer Maco.

MESSER MACO: I forgive you. Let's drop it.

Scene ii.
(MASTER ANDREA, MESSER MACO, *and* SANESE)

MASTER ANDREA: Are you looking for a master?

MESSER MACO: Yes sir.

SANESE: His name is Messer Maco de Coe . . .

MASTER ANDREA: No, no! I was asking whether you were looking for a master to serve.

SANESE: . . . and he turned twenty-two on the night of the Epiphany.

MASTER ANDREA: Let him speak, damn you!

MESSER MACO: Let me do the talking! It's very bad of you to speak before I do.

MASTER ANDREA: What did you come to Rome for?

SANESE: To see the *verbum caro*[38] and the jubilee.[39]

MESSER MACO: You don't know what you're talking about. I came here as a pope to find a place in the service of some emperor or king of France.

SANESE: You mean a cardinal in service to some pope.

MESSER MACO: You're right, Sanese.

MASTER ANDREA: You can't be a cardinal without becoming a courtier first. Now I'm an expert on the subject, and because of the love I have for the city, I'd be happy to do anything I can for you.

CORTIGIANA 61

MESSER MACO: *Ago vobis gratis.**
SANESE: Didn't I tell you? He's a scholar.
MASTER ANDREA: Your learning will bring you honor, especially among the Bergamese. But where are you staying?
MESSER MACO: In Rome.
MASTER ANDREA: Yes, yes, but I mean where in Rome?
SANESE: On a long, long street.
MASTER ANDREA: You're a credit to your master.
MESSER MACO: Wait — I have it on the tip of my tongue: botto ... scotto ... arlotto ... scarabotto ... biliotto ... Ceccotto ... Ceccotto![40] Ah! That's who we're staying with — a wise man, and a favorite of the Emperor.
MASTER ANDREA: My goodness! I'm happy to have met you. And as a token of our friendship I'll get you a book that teaches the art of courtier-making. It's the same book I used when I turned the Cardinal of Baccano, the Monsignore della Storta, and the Archbishop of Tre Capanne from beasts into men.[41]
MESSER MACO: Oh, please do that!
MASTER ANDREA: I'll be right back. I'll find you at Ceccotto's.
SANESE: What's your name?
MASTER ANDREA: Andrea, at Your Lordship's service.
SANESE: Of what? Where from?
MASTER ANDREA: S.P.Q.R.[42] I'm off.

Scene iii.
(MESSER MACO *and* SANESE)

MESSER MACO: *Bonum est nomen Magister Andreas.*†
SANESE: See, you're becoming what you wanted to be, just as it was prophesied.
MESSER MACO: What did you say?
SANESE: "Your Lordship ..." Didn't you hear Master Andrea call you "Your Lordship?"
MESSER MACO: I commend myself to Your Lordship.
SANESE: Fine. Now lift your cape.
MESSER MACO: Like this, Your Lordship?

---

* 'I am grateful to you.'
† 'That's a nice name: "Master Andrea."'

SANESE: Yes, Messer, wear your cap like this, walk along in a dignified way, like this . . . That's it—excellent!
MESSER MACO: Will I be a credit to the city?
SANESE: Damn it, of course you will!

Scene iv.
(A RASCAL *who sells books and papers)*

RASCAL: Read all about it! The Peace Between Christianity and the Emperor! The Capture of the King! *La riforma della corte,* written by the Bishop of Chieti! The *Caprici* of Brother Mariano, in *ottava rima.* An Eclogue by Trasinio! The Life of the Abbot of Gaeta! Fine stories! Splendid stories! *La Caretta*! *Il Cortigiano falito*! Get your stories here![43]

Scene v.
(MESSER MACO *and* SANESE)

MESSER MACO: Run and buy that book, Sanese, the one that'll teach me how to become a courtier. Run! Run!
SANESE: Hey there! Sell me the book that'll make this gentleman a courtier.

Scene vi.
(MESSER MACO, *alone*)

MESSER MACO: Look at that pretty lady up there, dressed in silk and leaning on the windowsill! She must surely be the wife of a King of Milan or a Duke of France. My goodness, I feel like I'm falling in love! What a beautiful street this is—there isn't a pebble in it!

Scene vii.
(SANESE, *alone*)

SANESE: This book cost me two *baiochi* . . . or *balochi* . . . whatever it is they call money in Rome![44] It's a good thing my master is next thing to a doctor, or he'd never in a thousand years understand the way they talk in this town. If I really knew how to read, this book would make me a courtier before my master, Maco da Coe of Siena. *O, madrama not vuole, o Lorenzina. Le star . . . starne . . . e . . . ne . . . .* They say *starne*; why don't they say *gallo* or *gallina*? . . . no, they say *starne*. Let's see: *e vado mendicano uno spe . . . speda . . . da . . . spedale . . .* (Why don't they say *palazzo*?) . . . so, when you put it all together, it's *spedale*, and it goes like this:

> *Le starne odiavi e or bramo una radice*
> *E vado mendicando uno spedale.**45

Christ! In Rome, you eat a root and you end up in a hospital! It'd have been better for me to stay in Siena as a Sienese than come to Rome as a courtier.

But where did my master go? Messer Maco! Maco! Master! Boss! Oh, no! Thieves have stolen him from me! Thieves! I'll get the magistrate to hang you! Hey you, you with the cap, where's my master?

See? No one answers me. I'd better have the town crier call for him and then get out of here.

Scene viii.
(MESSER MACO, *alone*)

MESSER MACO: Now I've lost my servant, and I barely managed to find my way back. I'd better figure out where I am. This is the door . . . no, this one . . . no, it must be this one. Oh, how can I manage without Sanese?

Scene ix.
(CAPPA *and* ROSSO, PARABOLANO's *servants*)

ROSSO: Our master is the most outrageous crook, the most incorrigible scoundrel, and the wickedest villain in the world. And barely three years ago he was just like us, trotting along as a footman.

CAPPA: I remember when he was a stableboy, and now he wouldn't condescend to touch the purest gold — not even with gloves on. If God himself were his servant, he still wouldn't be satisfied. He never shows his servants any consideration. He

---

*'I hate partridges, and I yearn for a root, and now I'm begging for a place to stay.'

hires them for a month at a time to see how they get along. A poor fellow will try to serve him the best he knows how so that he can stay with him, but at the end of the month he says, "You're not going to make it with me. I need someone who can do some heavy work. If there's anything I can do for you, let me know, but you're not for me."

ROSSO: I know what you mean. With dirty tricks like that he gets good service without having to pay any salaries.

CAPPA: It really bothers me: his valet takes more time to dress or undress him than it takes to get from one jubilee to the next. I blow my stack when I think that the bastard has a servant use a silver tray to bring him the paper to wipe his ass with — and before he takes it the servant has to bow to him. I wish he'd drop dead.

ROSSO: When he's at mass his page keeps track of his paternosters, and each time he says one, the page does a paternoster of his own, and makes a bow the way the Spanish do. It's the same way when he's at the font. First the boy — the one I mentioned — kisses his own finger, then he puts it into the holy water and presents it to his master. The clumsy clod touches the boy's finger and with great ceremony makes the sign of the cross on his own forehead.

CAPPA: Christ, that's worse than the Prior of Capua![46]

ROSSO: He can't scrape his feet, or comb his beard, or wash his hands, or mount his horse without a master of ceremonies.

CAPPA: How about hitting the bastard on the head some night with an ax?

ROSSO: Not that he doesn't deserve it, but let's wait and see. Maybe some day he'll change the way he treats us. In any case, something's bound to happen.

Scene x.

(The steward, VALERIO, *and the squire,* FLAMINIO*)*

VALERIO: Did you hear what they said?

FLAMINIO: You drunkards! Good-for-nothings! Thieves! Traitors! Is this the way to talk about your master?

Scene xi.
(ROSSO *and* VALERIO)

ROSSO: Boy, I sure made you jump, eh, Valerio? When Cappa and I realized you and Flaminio were listening, we started criticizing the Master — as a joke. But everybody knows what a great guy he is — and a perfect gentleman!

VALERIO: You have the gall to open your mouth, you shameless scoundrel! And you, Cappa — I wouldn't want to cheat the gallows, or I'd tear your heart out on the spot. Filthy gluttons! Off to your whorehouses . . . By God, I'd like to . . .

ROSSO: Please, take it easy!

Scene xii.
(FLAMINIO *and* VALERIO)

FLAMINIO: I swear, these noblemen, they don't deserve better servants than the likes of Rosso and Cappa. You're almost better off being like them than doing a proper job. I don't know how many times the Master's remarked to me how well behaved, and faithful, and polite Rosso is!

VALERIO: Polite? Sure, if liars, drunkards, backbiters, gluttons, thieves, and frauds are polite, then Rosso's an angel. Eh? What do you think? Look, if their noble lordships will swallow that kind of thing, then they'll call anyone well bred who can slice a pheasant, or make a neat bed or a graceful bow. A fellow like Rosso will get to be a big man at court before any scholar of Greek or Latin. A person like that, who stays on his master's good side by his talent for delivering messages, gets to be more arrogant than patience is humble. Oh, oh, oh, oh!

FLAMINIO: No more than an hour ago I heard about another master who was putting Julio down because he's a commoner. He said Parabolano was wrong to raise the status of a peasant like him just because of his ancient noble origins.

VALERIO: Flaminio, old man, in this day and age you can't just say, "Monsignor So-and-so, or Lord Such-and-such, is a relative of mine." Whether you're good or bad depends upon what you do yourself, not what your ancestors did. If noble blood were all that was needed to bring honor to men who don't deserve it, then the King of Cyprus and the Prince of Fiossa wouldn't be in such bad shape. Signor Constantino would get the principality of Macedonia back; he'd think it beneath his dignity to be governor of Fano.[47]

FLAMINIO: It's true—chronicles, and epitaphs, and privileges granted to your ancestors aren't of much use: Raphael the Jew[48] wouldn't lend two cents on aristocratic memories. Rome cares as much about nobility as Romanello[49] cares whether it's today or tomorrow that the Messiah's coming.

VALERIO: It's clear as can be. Fortune laughs at Greek or Trojan blood; more often than not cardinals and popes are born of the line of Ser Adriano.[50]

Scene xiii.
(PARABOLANO and VALERIO, *his steward*)

PARABOLANO: Valerio?
VALERIO: Yes, sir. Goodbye, Flaminio.
PARABOLANO: Call Rosso.
VALERIO: Oh sure, be nice to Rosso. The way he's just been talking about you, Hell will have to dream up new punishments for him.
PARABOLANO: My goodness, you take him too seriously! There's no shame in being criticized by someone like that, and no glory in being praised.
VALERIO: I'm perfectly aware of that. But the fact remains that you set people like him on a pedestal. There he is—look at the face on him!
PARABOLANO: Go inside and straighten up the room. And Rosso, you come with me.

Scene xiv.
(PARABOLANO and ROSSO)

PARABOLANO: Where have you been?
ROSSO: At the tavern, saving Your Lordship's honor, and I saw that tempting little piece, Angela Greca.
PARABOLANO: What was she doing?
ROSSO: She was talking to Don Cerimonia the Spaniard. They were talking about going to some vineyard for supper—I don't know which one—and I acted like Massino's cat.[51]

PARABOLANO: What did Massino's cat do?
ROSSO: She closed her eyes to keep from catching mice.
PARABOLANO: If only my other flame burnt as hot as that one, I'd have no problems.
ROSSO: When all's said and done, there's no point doing anything for a great lord, because everything ends up boring him.
PARABOLANO: Alas, my love will never bore me—she hardly even looks at me.
ROSSO: Didn't I tell you? You fill up too fast.
PARABOLANO: Be quiet now, and listen to me.
ROSSO: Speak up. I'm listening.
PARABOLANO: You know Messer Ceccotto's house?
ROSSO: That fool? Yes sir.
PARABOLANO: Foolish or wise, you'll go there and you'll take a present for Messer Maco, from Siena. His father treated my father very well when he studied in Siena. But I don't know what to send him.
ROSSO: Send him a few turtles.
PARABOLANO: Turtles? From someone like me? You dolt!
ROSSO: Send him a couple of nice Syrian kittens.
PARABOLANO: Can you eat cats, you rascal?
ROSSO: If you send him ten artichokes, he'll be your slave.
PARABOLANO: Devil take you! Where can you find artichokes at this time of year, you blockhead?
ROSSO: Give him two flasks of Mangiaguerra.[52] Riccio has some excellent stuff at the Hare.
PARABOLANO: Do you think he's a drunkard like you, you numbskull? Now get out of my hair. Take these ten scudi and buy some lampreys. Tell him . . . even though the gift is small, to eat them for the sake of our friendship. Try to find one or two decent words to say, won't you?
ROSSO: One or two? I'll say eighty thousand! It's a shame they don't send me as an ambassador to some Sophy. I'd bring honor on myself. I'd say to him, "Your Magnificence, Your Reverence, Your Sacred Majesty, Holy Father, Most Christian, Most Illustrious, Most Reverend *in Cristo Patri*,* Your Father-

---

*'In Christ the Father.'

hood, Your Almightiness, *Viro Domino*,*" and so on. And I'd make a bow, like this, and another one like this . . . I'd bow my head and everything.

PARABOLANO: Come on, hurry up, you big fool. But first bring this cape to Valerio. I'm going to the stable to look at those Arabian horses the Conte di Verucchio[53] sent me as a gift.

Scene xv.
(ROSSO, *alone*)

ROSSO: I'd like to see how I look in silk. I'd give anything for a mirror to see myself strutting around in these fancy clothes. After all, with a fine suit of clothes even a coat rack looks good. And most of these great lords would look like baboons or monkeys if they went around badly dressed. I should take off[54] with both the money and the clothes. I'm a real fool not to. I could stay a thousand years with this jerk, Parabolano, and never see a ducat. Besides, everyone would bless me for robbing one of these thieving masters—they rob us, body and soul. But why don't I cheat this fishmonger? That's a good idea. As far as that scoundrel my boss is concerned, I'll have lots better chances. And I want to try that trick that other fellow like me played—he was pretending to be shopping, and he sent a fishmonger to a friar confessor. Everybody knows the story.

Scene xvi.
(ROSSO [*dressed in the cape*] *and* FISHMONGER)

ROSSO: How many do you have left, not counting these?

FISHMONGER: None. Brother Mariano's steward just bought the rest.

ROSSO: You look like an honest fellow. Keep your whole catch for me: you're the one I'll be dealing with from now on.

FISHMONGER: My dear sir! Your Lordship! Please, please! I'd be delighted to serve you.

ROSSO: Fine, fine. What do you want for these?

---
*'Man God.'

FISHMONGER: Eight scudi . . . more or less . . . whatever Your Lordship would like to give me. Don't worry that I'm poor — I have a generous heart.

ROSSO: I'll give you six. Even at that price, I'd be paying more than they're worth.

FISHMONGER: Whatever you like, Your Lordship.

ROSSO: Dear, dear, would you look at how long it's taking my servants to get here with the mule! Those rascals! Those loafers! I'll send them to Ponte Sisto![55]

FISHMONGER: Don't upset yourself, sir. I'll deliver them.

ROSSO: Thank you. I told them to take the mule, but they must have thought I said the horse, and it's quite a job to saddle a fiery devil like that one.

FISHMONGER: I bet that's what's happened!

ROSSO: Let's go. We'll meet them on the way. What's your name?

FISHMONGER: Facenda. I'm a Florentine, from Porta Pinti. I live at San Pietro Gattolini. And I have two sisters at Borgo a la Noce, if it please Your Lordship.[56]

ROSSO: Get a pair of stockings made for yourself the color of my coat of arms.

FISHMONGER: Your Lordship's kindness is enough. Don't worry about anything else.

ROSSO: Whose side are you on, the Colonnas or the Ursini?[57]

FISHMONGER: To tell the truth, I'm on the side of whoever wins.

ROSSO: You're a wise man. Make sure that the left one's a solid color and the right one is striped.

FISHMONGER: I'll do that, just as Your Lordship wishes.

ROSSO: Get some one to paint my crest on your stall.

FISHMONGER: What's your crest?

ROSSO: A golden ladder on a blue field. But isn't that just my luck! I have a few ducats on me, but not what I need. There's my steward over there, at the door of St. Peter's. See him? He'll pay you.

FISHMONGER: Just in time. That's lucky.

ROSSO: Wait for me here. I'll be right back.

Scene xvii.
(ROSSO and SACRISTAN)

ROSSO: Father, you see that poor wretch over there? His wife is possessed, and she's doing crazy things down at the Luna. I beg you, Father, chain her to this column and in the name of God take this curse from her. She's got maybe ten spirits in her body, speaking every language under the sun, and the poor man is half crazy.

Scene xviii.
SACRISTAN, ROSSO, and FISHMONGER

SACRISTAN: He's coming over. Look, I have a few words to say to this friend of mine, then I'll be glad to do whatever I have to.

FISHMONGER: Thank you, Father.

ROSSO: Now don't you worry. Give me the lampreys, and take these four julios as a down payment for the stocking-maker.

FISHMONGER: You're doing too much, Your Lordship. But which stocking is to be striped?

ROSSO: Whichever you like.

FISHMONGER: Good. A man could starve waiting for this damned steward. Hurry up, cancer take you! Talk, talk, talk! Well, so long as he pays me royally for my time. I'd have taken four scudi for them, but you're giving me eight! Great stewards, eh? And wonderful managers!

Scene xix.
(SACRISTAN and FISHMONGER)

SACRISTAN: Hey! Can't you hear?

FISHMONGER: I'm right here, Your Lordship's servant.

SACRISTAN: Now don't worry. I'm here to help you.

FISHMONGER: If Your Lordship does anything for me, it will be like alms to a beggar. I have four little children, and not one of them weighs more than any of the others.

SACRISTAN: When did they enter?

FISHMONGER: Four.

SACRISTAN: During the day or the night?

FISHMONGER: Between last night and this morning.

SACRISTAN: And the name?
FISHMONGER: You don't know? They're lampreys.
SACRISTAN: No, no — I'm asking your wife's name, and how many spirits have possessed her.
FISHMONGER: Go ahead, have a good time, and God bless you for it. But if you had to worry about your bread, it'd be no joking matter.
SACRISTAN: Your father must have put a curse on you.
FISHMONGER: My father put a curse on me when he left me poor.
SACRISTAN: Have San Gregorio's masses[58] said for him.
FISHMONGER: I'll have . . . I'd better not say it. What the devil do San Gregorio's masses have to do with lampreys? Steward, I want to get paid; if not, I'll complain to the Pope himself.
SACRISTAN: Hold him, priests! Stay still! *Qui habitat!*[*] Cross yourselves.
FISHMONGER: Christ! Let go of me, you damned priests!
SACRISTAN: You're biting me! Demon, I exorcise you!
FISHMONGER: Using your fists, eh, you bastards?
SACRISTAN: Drag him into the church — to the holy water.
FISHMONGER: Me? Possessed? Me? I could kill you!
SACRISTAN: You will leave this man without doing any injury, *in aiutorio altissimi!*[†] Wherein will you enter? Answer me!
FISHMONGER: Up your ass, that's where! Up your ass! You got that?

Scene xx.
(CAPPA *and* ROSSO)

CAPPA: You seem very happy, Rosso, laughing away to yourself. What's going on?
ROSSO: I've just got to laugh! I played this joke so neatly, the trickmaster himself couldn't have done it better. When I have time I'll tell you about it. Right now I've got to bring this cape to my master, and then make a present of these lampreys to a gentleman. I'll meet you later at the Hare.
CAPPA: Hurry back.

---

[*] 'It is here that he dwells.'

[†] 'In the name of the highest helper.'

ROSSO: Yes, yes. Right away.

Scene xxi.
(FISHMONGER *and* CAPPA)

FISHMONGER: Rome's too much for me. Anyone who thinks it's paradise must be joking!

CAPPA: What's the matter, Facenda?

FISHMONGER: What lousy tricks they play in Rome! And who to? To a Florentine! Imagine what they'd do to a Sienese! And every day you hear about some new law forbidding us to carry arms!

CAPPA: What's the trouble? Can't you tell me?

FISHMONGER: Sure I can tell you. The way I've been cheated out of some lampreys — well, I'm ashamed to talk about it. And then they chained me to the column as if I were possessed. "Put out the lamp." "Knock on the door." "Don't hurt anyone." I've taken so many punches that all my hair's fallen out. Cuckold priests, sodomites, thieves! By the body . . . by the blood . . . If I get my hands on that pig of a Sacristan I'll eat his nose off! I'll bash his eyes in! I'll tear out his tongue! Damn Rome, the court, the church, everyone who lives here, and everyone who believes in it!

CAPPA: My God, this must have been one hell of a swindle! I almost feel as if it happened to me! If there's anything I can do, just ask me.

FISHMONGER: Thanks, but I just want to get out of Rome! I want to leave the filthy place. If I ever find someone from here in Florence . . . well, I might just . . . I might . . . yes . . . yes . . .

Scene xxii.
(PARABOLANO *and* VALERIO)

PARABOLANO: Oh, how hateful life's beginning to be!

VALERIO: It's for poor servants like us that life is really hateful.

PARABOLANO: You can't feel the cause of my suffering.

VALERIO: More often than not you suffer because you're too well off. It really bothers me to hear someone like you complaining. Think about a person like me, living on someone else's bread:

what should I do? If I so much as stumbled over a piece of straw I'd break my neck!

PARABOLANO: I don't understand.

VALERIO: If you were like a lot of servants who balance their hopes on the scales of some priest's whim, then you'd understand.

PARABOLANO: Oh envious fortune!

VALERIO: Fortune? You nobles are the fortunate ones — in fact, you're the ones who control fortune! You raise up vice and ignorance from the stables, and then down into the stables you throw virtue.

PARABOLANO: I'm wasting away!

VALERIO: What do you want?

PARABOLANO: The reward for my labours.

VALERIO: Who do you want it from?

PARABOLANO: Where am I? If only I could receive some letters, some messages.

VALERIO: Where should these letters be addressed to?

PARABOLANO: Wherever I am.

VALERIO: You'd be late getting them.

PARABOLANO: Why?

VALERIO: Because it seems to me you're neither here nor there.

PARABOLANO: Help me.

VALERIO: I can't help you if you don't tell me your secret.

PARABOLANO: How many bitter poisons are hidden in precious vessels! Let's go inside.

Scene xxiii.
(MASTER ANDREA, *alone*)

MASTER ANDREA: First I volunteer to find a master for this Sienese, then I set myself up as his teacher. What do you think of that? Well now, if I'm so smart I guess I'd better get on with it, and by August I'll have him all sewed up. And if this works, I'll do a job on my father as well. Anyone who wants his brains sent through the mail, I'd be glad to pay for the horses. I think the greatest act of charity in the world would be to drive someone crazy, maybe by giving him an office or a benefice. No sooner do his brains leave him but his head's filled with power, and splendor, and triumphs, and gardens that bloom like rosemary at every change of the moon. These people get such a charge when you say you believe them, or flatter them, or agree with anything they say! By God, people like that wouldn't trade their situation for the one the Emperor gave to Ceccotto.[59] But there's that big prick my pupil standing at the door like a boundary post. I swear, as soon as I find the master of the revels I'm going to have him placed on the catalogue of fools, so that he can be solemnly commemorated, to the glory and honor of the most reverend and imperial city of Siena.

Scene xxiv.
(MESSER MACO *and* MASTER ANDREA)

MASTER ANDREA: Welcome, Your Lordship.

MESSER MACO: Oh, good evening, and good year! Am I glad to see you! I lost my servant, and now I thought I'd lost you, too.

MASTER ANDREA: It'd be better to lose me for good than just misplace me. Now here's your book. Let's go inside and I'll give you a lesson. Because it's the first time, it'll be short and sweet.

MESSER MACO: Please, Master, do me a favor and teach me a bit of courtiership right now.

MASTER ANDREA: Gladly. Open your eyes — wide. The first, most important lessons a good courtier learns are how to blaspheme and how to commit heresy.

MESSER MACO: Oh no, I won't do that. I'd go to hell. That would be bad for me.

MASTER ANDREA: Hell? What do you mean? Surely you know that here in Rome there's no need to break your neck keeping Lent!

MESSER MACO: Is that right?

MASTER ANDREA: Of course! Look, everyone who comes to Rome, the moment they get to court, they want to look as if they've been around: they wouldn't go to mass for all the gold in the world. And if they do, they never open their mouths without swearing on the Madonna and the Sacred Host.

MESSER MACO: Well then . . . I'll curse the cunt of Modena. How's that?

MASTER ANDREA: Fine.

MESSER MACO: But how do you get to be a heretic? That's a tricky one.
MASTER ANDREA: When someone tells you ostriches are camels, say "I don't believe it."
MESSER MACO: I don't believe it.
MASTER ANDREA: And when someone tells you that priests have any common sense, scoff at them.
MESSER MACO: I scoff at them.
MASTER ANDREA: And when someone tells you there's any conscience in Rome, laugh at them.
MESSER MACO: Ha, ha, ha!
MASTER ANDREA: In short, whenever you hear someone saying anything good about the Roman court, tell him he's not telling the truth.
MESSER MACO: Wouldn't it be better to say "You're lying in your teeth!"?
MASTER ANDREA: Great! That would be quicker and shorter! That's enough for the first lesson. Later I'll teach you about the Barco, the Botte de Termini, the Colosseum, the arches, Testaccio, and thousands of other fine things that a blind man would give an eye to see.[60]
MESSER MACO: What's a Colosseum? Is it sweet or bitter?
MASTER ANDREA: It's the sweetest thing in Rome, and everyone loves it, because it's an antiquity.
MESSER MACO: I know about the arches because of the chronicles, and I've seen them written about in the Bible. It's the same with antiquities. But must all antiquities be grottoes?
MASTER ANDREA: Yes and no. As you find out about these matters you'll get to know Master Pasquino.[61] But you'll find it's no easy job getting to know who Master Pasquino really is. He's got a sharp tongue.
MESSER MACO: What's his trade, this Master Pasquino?
MASTER ANDREA: He's a poet who plays filthy songs on the rebec.[62]
MESSER MACO: A poet? What do you mean, poet? I know all the poets by heart, and I'm a poet myself.
MASTER ANDREA: Really?
MESSER MACO: Sure! Listen to this epigram I wrote in praise of myself.

MASTER ANDREA: Go ahead.
MESSER MACO:
> Si deus est animas prima cupientibus artem
> Silvestrem tenui noli gaudere malorum
> Hanc tua Penelope nimium ne crede colori
> Tityre tu patule numerum sine viribus uxor.*

MASTER ANDREA: Oh, mercy! What style!
MESSER MACO:
> Mortem repentina pleno semel orbe cohissent
> Tres sumus in bello vaccinia nigra leguntur
> O formose puer musam meditaris avena
> Dic michi Dameta recumbans sub termine fagi . . .†

MASTER ANDREA: What a rich vein of foolishness!
MESSER MACO: Aren't I clever, Master?
MASTER ANDREA: Cleverer than usury, which can teach you to read your pawn tickets! My goodness, if you were to give me these songs I'd be rich! I'd have them printed by Ludovico Vicintino and Lautizio da Perugia[63] and I'd be rich as a king. But since you've lost your page, we must find you another one, because I want you to fall in love!
MESSER MACO: I'm already in love with a lady, and I'm rich, and whatever you want me to do, I'll do it.
MASTER ANDREA: Since you're rich, we'll get you a house and some clothes. You'll buy horses, and we'll have masked banquets in the vineyards. Go along now, my most magnificent sir! Ha, ha, ha, ha!

---

*'If it was a god who first coveted the sylvan art
Do not rejoice in the tender ills;
And do not trust overmuch your Penelope's complexion,
Tityrus, you husband with a calendar, for your wife is without men.'

†'Sudden death brings the world full circle.
There are three of us in the fight to tie up the black calf.
O gorgeous boy, with your pipe you meditate upon the muse.
Tell me, Dameta, reclining in the shade of a beech tree . . .'

Act II

Scene i.
(ROSSO *and* CAPPA)

ROSSO: If you've never been to a tavern, you don't know what paradise is! What a friendly place! People can make a name for themselves here. O sweet tavern, you do whatever anyone asks — you'd think we were all lords. And look at how everyone bows to you! By God, Cappa, if I had any children I'd send them to the tavern to teach them how to behave — how to get along in life.

CAPPA: You're a smart fellow!

ROSSO: Ah, that lovely music the spits make when they're crammed with thrushes, or sausages, or capons! Ah, the aroma of suckling calf, stuffed with succulent spices!

CAPPA: Right! If there were taverns next door to perfume shops, people would be turned off civet.

ROSSO: There are some dumb oxen who make a big thing about how sweet it is to love and to make love. I'll tell you what's sweet: having a good feed, without all that sighing and jealousy. You know Caesar, who the boss admires so much? Now if he'd just had himself a good time in a tavern, with everything set up just right, he'd have got fed up with his triumphal arches, I'm sure of it; but on the other hand his soldiers would have been more willing to go through them.

CAPPA: I can believe it.

ROSSO: The splendor of it! What a joy it is to see steaming roasts, and all kinds of fish! There's nothing like the sight of a well-stocked table! If I'd been that pope who built the Belvedere,[64] with its splendid view, I'd have spent all my money in a tavern. Talk about beautiful views! I'd have a wonderful view of something every month or so, and it wouldn't be loggias or painted chambers.

CAPPA: Rosso, these lampreys are fit for an angel! Now me, I don't begrudge anyone leaving the stables to become a nobleman; but when I see guys like Brandino or the Morro de' Nobili[65] stuffing their guts with heavenly, divine morsels like these, I want to explode — it turns my stomach — I can't breathe!

ROSSO: Sure they're delicious, everyone knows that, but if that fishmonger of mine finds me, he'll see that I digest them in a hurry.

CAPPA: Let him do what he wants. I've never been a fighter, but I'd die a hundred times a day for one of these lampreys. But there's Valerio calling for you. See you later.

Scene ii.
(MESSER MACO, MASTER ANDREA, *and* GRILLO, *servant of* MESSER MACO)

MASTER ANDREA: This robe looks good on you. You're like a paladin.

MESSER MACO: Come on! Don't make me laugh!

MASTER ANDREA: Have you managed to learn what I taught you?

MESSER MACO: I can do anyone.

MASTER ANDREA: Do me a duke.

MESSER MACO: This way . . . Like this . . . and this . . . Whoops! I fell!

MASTER ANDREA: Get up, blockhead!

MESSER MACO: Make me two eyeholes in the cape. I can't do a duke in the dark.

MASTER ANDREA: O.K. now, how would you address a gentleman?

MESSER MACO: I kiss your hand.

MASTER ANDREA: And a lady?

MESSER MACO: Thy heart is mine!

MASTER ANDREA: A good friend?

MESSER MACO: Ah, by my faith!

MASTER ANDREA: A priest?

MESSER MACO: I swear to God.

MASTER ANDREA: Good! Well done! And a servant—show me how you'd give an order.
MESSER MACO: Bring me my mule and lay out my clothes, or I'll kill you!
GRILLO: Tell him to let me go, Master Andrea. I don't work for roughnecks like him!
MESSER MACO: It's only a joke, Grillo. I'm learning how to be a courtier. I won't hurt you.
MASTER ANDREA: Let's go now. You've got to learn about Borgo Vecchio, Corte Savella, Torre di Nona, Ponte Sisto, and Dietro Banchi.[66]
MESSER MACO: Does Borgo Vecchio have a beard?
MASTER ANDREA: Ha, ha, ha!
MESSER MACO: Does Torre de Nona ring vespers as well?
MASTER ANDREA: With a few pulls of the rope for compline, too! Then we'll visit St. Peter's, where you'll see the pine cone, the ship, the Camposanto, and the obelisk.[67]
MESSER MACO: Can we go into the Camposanto with our shoes on?
MASTER ANDREA: You can, yes; others, no.
MESSER MACO: Let's go. I want to eat that cone, and I don't care what it costs.

Scene iii.
(ROSSO, *alone*)

ROSSO: That stupid master of mine thinks I don't know why he's acting so strangely—and I pretended not to know what's eating him. When I was taking my usual walk through the house last night, I heard him talking in his sleep; he was having it on with Lady Laura, Messer Luzio's wife. He was calling her by name and caressing her just as though she were there. This is my secret—I haven't told anyone. I'll pass off the bawd Aloigia as her nurse, and that way I'll make the Master believe whatever I want. I'm off to see her now. I bet she could corrupt chastity itself. She'll do anything I want, because she loves me.

Scene iv.
(PARABOLANO, *alone*)

PARABOLANO: I'd rather die than live like this. When I was a nobody, the itch to climb the ladder bothered me twenty-four hours a day. And now that I'm just about content with my position I'm taken with a horrible fever that no medicine can cure. Except one. And that's a medicine you can't buy no matter how rich or important you are, because it's only sold by the god of Love, and the price he asks is the blood, the tears, even the death of his subjects. O Love, what can you not do! You're much more powerful than Fortune. She governs only men; you command both men and gods! She is fickle and inconstant. . . . What with women's weapons like those and this suffering of mine, I'll never win her, though I want her more than life itself. I must go to my room. Maybe Love will teach me how to free myself, just as it taught me to get myself all tangled up. Then again, maybe I could make my own escape from this torment—with stone, or steel, or rope, or poison!

Scene v.
(FLAMINIO *and old* SEMPRONIO)

SEMPRONIO: Would you advise me, then, to place my son Camillo in service at court?

FLAMINIO: Yes, if he's an enemy of yours and you hate him.

SEMPRONIO: The court has declined a lot in the time that you've been a courtier. Why I remember when I was with the most reverend Monsignor, there was nothing like it—it was a paradise! We were a band of brothers, each of us rich and each one a favorite.

FLAMINIO: You old folks followed the old rules, but by the Lord Harry, we're living in modern times! In your day, a servant of Pope John[68] would be given a bed, a room, his wood, his candles, and his horse, and they'd pay for his washerwoman, his barber, his servant, and every year two new suits of clothes. Nowadays, no sooner is a poor courtier accepted than he has to look after his own fire and water—and even when they take you under their wing, they only give you half a servant.

Think about it. Can a whole man get along with half a servant? The only thing to be said for them is that if you get sick when you're in their service, they'll put you in the hospital with lots of recommendations.

SEMPRONIO: What do they do, with so much money coming in?

FLAMINIO: They go to whores and boys. But they die before they've really satisfied their lusts, and then they leave fifteen or twenty thousand scudi to the kind of people who don't care a fart for their souls.

SEMPRONIO: But that's madness!

FLAMINIO: It wouldn't be so bad if they treated their servants well. But do you know what those clowns do?

SEMPRONIO: No, I don't.

FLAMINIO: They've learned to eat by themselves in their rooms. They'll tell you it's because it would be the death of them to eat two full meals a day — and that they eat very little at night. But the reason the skinflints do it is so they won't have to invite poor deserving men of talent to have dinner with them.

SEMPRONIO: That's shameful! What a terrible thing to do!

FLAMINIO: There's a great story about the Bishop of Malfetta.[69] His steward had paid a couple of pennies more than usual for a fish, so he didn't want it. The steward and some of the servants pooled their money and bought it. While they were cooking it to eat it together, the good bishop smelled it and ran to the kitchen; he wanted to pay his share and eat some of it, but the fine fellows wouldn't go for that.

SEMPRONIO: Ha, ha, he, he, oh, ho, ho!

FLAMINIO: Here's a better one. I heard at Ponzetta's[70] that there was a most reverend Monsignor who used to have them put an egg and a half in each omelette, and then he'd put it in one of those forms that keep cardinals' hats in the proper shape. Now one morning a strange thing happened: the wind carried them, like the leaves of autumn, to the steps of St. Peter's, and they fell like crowns upon the heads of the people.

SEMPRONIO: Ha, ha, ha!

FLAMINIO: Listen — here's another one. You used to have men as chamberlains; well we have women: our masters' mothers. They're always giving us trouble: they taste the wines and see if there's enough water. They keep the keys of the wine cellars and they ration the food — so much on feast days, so much on regular days. They even count the bowls of soup!

SEMPRONIO: Well I'm sure my son wouldn't stay in a house like that!

FLAMINIO: Once he's a courtier, he'll become an envious, ambitious, wretched, ungrateful flatterer, a wicked, unjust, heretical hypocrite, a thief, an insolent lying glutton; and . . . well, what's the mildest vice there is? Treachery? Well then, treachery's the mildest vice you'll find there.

SEMPRONIO: What? You mean there are thieves even at court?

FLAMINIO: Thieves? Sure there are! And the least thing they rob you of is ten or twenty years of life and service. And you're always waiting for somebody to die — it doesn't matter who. Let's say that the one you hoped would make way for you survives. Then, unhappy wretch, you're tormented by all that vexation, all those fevers and sufferings you went through during the sickness of the one whose death was going to make you rich, because now he's in good health. It's a cruel thing to wish for the death of someone who never did you any harm.

SEMPRONIO: May God forsake me if my Camillo ever serves at court.

FLAMINIO: Sempronio, if you're asking my advice so that I'll tell you what you want to hear, that's one thing, but if you want me to tell you the truth that's another matter.

SEMPRONIO: I'm most obliged to you, Flaminio, and I know you're a good and honest man. I'm determined not to send my son into anyone's service — we'll talk about this some more when we have the time. I've got to go pick up my pay from the Strozzi Bank[71] for some services I did.

FLAMINIO: And I'll go back to court and waste away with bitterness.

Scene vi.
(ROSSO *and* ALOIGIA, *a bawd*)

ROSSO: Where are you going in such a hurry?

ALOIGIA: Oh, here and there — the usual worries.

ROSSO: What have you got to complain about? You've got Rome under your thumb!

ALOIGIA: Maybe so, but my dear old mentor's troubles have really shaken me.
ROSSO: What's the matter? Is she sick?
ALOIGIA: She'll be sick all right — and all because of her goodness. They're burning her tomorrow morning. I ask you, is that fair?
ROSSO: It's not fair, and it's not decent. Why the devil are they burning her? Did she crucify Jesus or something?
ALOIGIA: She hasn't done anything.
ROSSO: What, do they burn people for doing nothing? What is this? Thievery! Corruption! Take it from me, Rome's on the road to ruin.
ALOIGIA: She loved her *comare*'s baby so much that she drowned it.
ROSSO: Is that all?
ALOIGIA: She cast a spell on her *compare* as a favor to a friend.
ROSSO: That's what I call style!
ALOIGIA: She poisoned Georgina's husband because he was such a loser.
ROSSO: The magistrate couldn't take a joke.
ALOIGIA: Rosso, my dear, she's made the will of a queen — I'll inherit everything she has.
ROSSO: Wonderful! What did she leave you? Can you tell me?
ALOIGIA: Lots of lovely things: alembics for distilling, washes to take away freckles and the scars from the French disease, a strap to lift sagging breasts, tweezers for plucking eyelashes, a flask of lovers' tears, a glass of bats' blood, dead men's bones, for torments and betrayals, owls' claws, vultures' hearts, wolves' teeth, bears' fat, ropes from people who've been hanged by mistake. That's all they talk about in the neighborhood. And then thanks to her I'm the one they call on to clean their teeth and get rid of stinking breath, and do a thousand other services.
ROSSO: Free her soul by fasting, and have them say San Gregorio's masses and St. Julian's paternosters,[72] and any other prayers that might do her good.
ALOIGIA: As if I wouldn't do that if she needs me to! The poor dear thing!
ROSSO: Crying won't get her back.
ALOIGIA: Even policemen raised their caps to her. It breaks my heart when I think of it. And it was hardly a month ago, at

the Peacock, that she drank off six mugs of wine right from the jug without batting an eyelash! She was the best friend anyone ever had. There was never an old woman who ate so much and worked so little.

ROSSO: And so Death wants her for himself.

ALOIGIA: Whether she was at the butcher's, the deli, the market, or the fair; by the river; at the bakery, or the baths, or the barber's, or the tollhouse, or the tavern; with policemen, or cooks, or messengers, or priests, or friars, or soldiers, they always expected her to say her piece. Everyone considered her a Solomon.

ROSSO: Burn them! Hang them! There's not a good man or woman left!

ALOIGIA: She was like a she-dragon, an amazon—she'd pluck out hanged men's eyes, or at night in the graveyards she'd pull the fingernails off corpses to make a cure for the colic. She'd change herself into a cat, or a mouse, or a dog, and she'd fly over the water, riding the wind all the way to the walnut tree in Benevento.[73]

ROSSO: What's her name?

ALOIGIA: Madonna Maggiorina, God forgive me.[74] Don't cross yourself—you heard it right!

ROSSO: Is this the way they do justice in Rome? Oh, oh, oh, oh! This is too much!

ALOIGIA: You're a good man. That's why you feel sorry.

ROSSO: If this were the middle of August, I'd have her name called through every quarter of the city by Rienzo Capovacina, or by Lielo, the chief of the Parione gang.[75]

ALOIGIA: If they just clipped our ears and noses and paraded us around with mitres on our heads, we could live with it. I went through it myself when I was a youngster. After all, it's not much more than a fleabite—and anyway, you've got to go through things like that up here so as not to go down there to the hot place.

ROSSO: That's true. Those priests who were drawn and quartered—what gave them the patience they needed was a good drink of wine.

ALOIGIA: That was another dirty trick. And weren't they sworn brothers of my dear mentor?

ROSSO: Let's drop the subject before we lose our tempers. Let's talk about something cheerful, because we're going to die too, and God knows whether it will be better or worse. Cheer up, Aloigia. My master's in love with Messer Luzio's Laura.

ALOIGIA: He's my foster brother.

ROSSO: We're rich! He's never told anyone — it was while he was dreaming that I heard him say it. I'd like ...

ALOIGIA: Quiet — leave it to me. You want him to believe that she's pining away for him.

ROSSO: Let's go inside. You're as welcome as a privy to someone who's taken a dose of salts.

Scene vii.
(MESSER MACO *and* MASTER ANDREA)

MESSER MACO: You mean that bronze pine cone is made of wood?

MASTER ANDREA: Yes sir.

MESSER MACO: That ship with the drowning saints — what's that?

MASTER ANDREA: It's a mosaic ...

MESSER MACO: Oh yes, music. Have her teach me music — it's important if I'm to become a courtier. Although I already know the staff and the scale: *re be mi mi fa sol fa re.*

MASTER ANDREA: You've got a good start on it; but now it would be a good idea to go have a rest.

MESSER MACO: I'm awfully thirsty, God forgive me.

MASTER ANDREA: Here's the house. After you, sir.

MESSER MACO: You go ahead — you're the teacher.

MASTER ANDREA: You go first, sir.

MESSER MACO: *Non bene conveniunt.*[*] With your permission.

Scene viii.
(PARABOLANO *and* VALERIO)

PARABOLANO: Shall I speak, or hold my peace? If I speak, she will scorn me, but if I remain silent, I will die. If I write to her declaring my love, she will be angry to find herself loved by a man of low estate. If I say nothing, the concealment of such

---
[*] 'It's not the right thing, but ...'

passion will lead to my death. O God of Love, be thou my counsellor.

VALERIO: Sir, I don't want to be presumptuous, but if I'm to serve you properly I must know what's bothering you. Then I'll stake my life on finding an answer to your problem.

PARABOLANO: I know, you've always been like that. That's why you've become what you are to me. But as for this latest misfortune of mine, you don't need to know about it.

VALERIO: That's not worthy of a man of your position. It's little credit to you that a base desire should so completely overcome your common sense. You may try to hide it, but it's easy to see that you're suffering the effects of love: you eat little; you're not sleeping at all; your passions are painted on your face. But if it is love, don't you have the courage to win whatever woman you want? You're rich, handsome, noble, generous, and shrewd, and you have a smooth tongue. A man with talents like these could win Venus herself, let alone a woman who's pierced your heart the way this one has.

PARABOLANO: If wise words were salves to cure my wounds, you'd have healed me by now.

VALERIO: Please, sir, pull yourself together. Is this really you? You're not yourself. Stop acting so strangely. You don't want the court and all your followers talking about you. And do you want them to know about this shameful foolishness in Naples? It will bring you shame; it will be the death of you. Do you think your family would be pleased to hear such a thing about you? What glory would it bring to your country? What comfort to your friends? What profit to us poor servants?

PARABOLANO: Go take a walk! You'll have me flying off the handle if you don't stop jabbering!

Scene ix.

(PARABOLANO, *alone*)

PARABOLANO: I know that what Valerio says is true—he's a very sensible young fellow. But I'm so much in love that I can't get over it. Yet I know that everything comes to an end. Today is different from yesterday; ice and snow don't last forever;

eventually the gods and the heavens are satisfied. It'll be better if I follow Valerio's advice. There he is at the door. Valerio!

Scene x.
(PARABOLANO *and* VALERIO)

PARABOLANO: Valerio, if I were in love as you say I am, what remedy would you give me?

VALERIO: Find a go-between and write a letter.

PARABOLANO: What if she refuses it?

VALERIO: You can be sure that a woman will never refuse either letters or cash.

PARABOLANO: What should I tell her?

VALERIO: Follow Love's dictation.

PARABOLANO: What if she takes it the wrong way?

VALERIO: Remember: women's flesh is more tender than ours, and their bones are softer.

PARABOLANO: When would you send the letter?

VALERIO: I'd wait for an opportune moment.

PARABOLANO: I sure got you talking, didn't I? Well it's not love that's bothering me.

VALERIO: If it had been up to you, Master, the fortress of San Leo would never have been captured;[76] you don't even have the courage to win a woman.

PARABOLANO: This doesn't make me feel one little bit better. Now let's go inside. I don't want to talk to anyone. I'd rather be by myself.

Scene xi.
(MASTER ANDREA, *alone*)

MASTER ANDREA: Messer Meathead has been drinking, and he's fallen in love with Camilla Pisana after seeing her through her chamber windows. This is one of those times when Cupid becomes stupid. He sings extempore and composes the most wretched verses. They're the most disgusting lyrics you've ever heard. And so that you won't take me for a liar, like the astrologers who are always predicting the flood, I'd like to read you a letter he's sending to the lady.

(*Letter from* MESSER MACO *to* CAMILLA PISANA)

"Hail, queen of mercies. Your marble eyes, your glittering mouth, your snaky hair, your coral brow, and your brocaded lips have turned me inside out, and so I've come to Rome, and, *favente deo*,[*] for the sake of your love I'll become a courtier, because you are softer than ricotta, cooler than ice, shinier than mandrake, sweeter than the full moon, and more beautiful than Fata Morgana[77] or the Morning Star. So search out the time and await the place where I can say a thousand words to you, which will be as secret as a proclamation and *fiat voluntas tua*.[†]

Maco, whose suff'ring for you makes him sick,
He has to have you, quick, quick, quick, quick, quick!"

Scene xii.
(MESSER MACO *and* MASTER ANDREA)

MESSER MACO: Take this little poem along too.
MASTER ANDREA: Gladly. But I want to read it first, because you're a tricky devil. How do I know you're not telling them to give me a hundred lashes?
MESSER MACO: No, no, Master, I'm fond of you.
MASTER ANDREA: Oh, I'm sure you are.

(*A strambottino*[78] *by* MESSER MACO, *read by* MASTER ANDREA)

O little star of love! O angel's courtier!
O carven image! Visage oriental!
I ache to sail my ship into your port; you're
More lovely far than all that's occidental.

Your glorious beauties came to us from France,
Like Judas, who did on his rope expire.
For love of you, as courtier I'll advance.
I wait for you in transports of desire.

---
[*]'God willing.'
[†]'May your will be done.'

Oh how full of meaning your verses are, how terse, how polished, how learned, how original, how witty, how divine, how fluent, how sweet, how succulent! But there's one little phrase that's not quite right.
MESSER MACO: What? The ship in the port?
MASTER ANDREA: Yes sir.
MESSER MACO: It's poetic licence. Now to my goddess. Off you go! Quickly!

Scene xiii.
(MASTER ANDREA, *alone*)

MASTER ANDREA: Poetry is really taking a bath today! We'll have to saddle a camel for Messer Maco and crown him with thorns, and nettles, and beets; laurels and myrtles make a big fuss before they'll grace anyone's temples — it's only emperors, poets, and taverns they'll condescend to decorate. But it looks as if we'll have to put Messer Maco in a straitjacket for two or three months or he'll go crazy with joy — he'll explode! Now let's go find Zoppino.

Scene xiv.
(ROSSO, *alone*)

ROSSO: The old woman will do what she has to. Oh, she's a tough one, this Aloigia. She has more tricks up her sleeve than the stitches of a thousand tailors. She's a bearded witch, Satan's mother-in-law, the devil's wife, the mother of the AntiChrist! But let her be what she wants; as for me, all I need is to bump off my boss and get my own back for the thousands of pointless troubles the little twerp has caused me. He may think of himself as about twenty-two come April or May, but he's over forty. He thinks that all the duchesses in the world are pining away for him, but it's the baker's wife he'll be tasting, the big ignoramus! Here he comes.

Scene xv.
(ROSSO *and* PARABOLANO)

PARABOLANO: What's new, Rosso?

ROSSO: I'd like you to have a little laugh—just for me.

PARABOLANO: All right.

ROSSO: There's a bad word that's written everywhere; no one knows who writes it, and it's never been spoken by a happy man.

PARABOLANO: Anything more?

ROSSO: Look here, let's get back to the point. What would you pay me if I were to guess how love tortures you, and for whom? It's not the wine that gave me this gift of prophecy—it tastes like water, thank God, so that my mind is clear as a bell.

PARABOLANO: What are you talking about, brother?

ROSSO: Brother, eh? Listen—I know her name, whose wife she is, where she lives, everything.

PARABOLANO: What? Her house, her husband, herself?

ROSSO: Everything: wife, husband, nurse, kids—and worse.

PARABOLANO: If you can tell me the first letter of her name, you've earned yourself a hundred ducats.

ROSSO: Gold ducats or cheap ones?[79]

PARABOLANO: Gold.

ROSSO: Large or small?

PARABOLANO: Large—and lots of them!

ROSSO: Get me out of the servants' quarters and I'll tell you everything—although you don't deserve it.

PARABOLANO: I'll make you chamberlain. Does it begin with an *S*?

ROSSO: No sir.

PARABOLANO: An *A*?

ROSSO: Right! Just like Viola!

PARABOLANO: With a *Z*?

ROSSO: Santa Luna is a little higher.

PARABOLANO: With a *C*?

ROSSO: You're looking through a peephole! Look—tomorrow or next day I'll be glad to tell you.

PARABOLANO: Dear God, how can you stand by and let a servant torment me?

ROSSO: What does it matter whether you find out today or tomorrow? After all, even if you murder Laura, you'll still have Rosso at your service, and he's as valiant as Astolfo.[80]

PARABOLANO: Stop it! Where am I?

ROSSO: In ecstasy!
PARABOLANO: Am I asleep?
ROSSO: Yes, as far as doing me any good is concerned.
PARABOLANO: Who am I talking to?
ROSSO: Rosso, who's not going to be eating in the servants' hall any more. To me that sounds better than if I were *podestà* of Norcia, ambassador to Todi, and Viceroy of Baccano.[81]
PARABOLANO: Let's go inside, my dearest friend. It'll be worth your while.

Scene xvi.
(ZOPPINO, *a pimp, and* MASTER ANDREA)

MASTER ANDREA: No one's had this much fun since jokes were first invented.
ZOPPINO: I'll tell him that the lady sent me to call on his highness, and if it weren't for her respect for the Spaniard, Don Lindezza, who's so jealous that he keeps guards at her door night and day, he could come and sleep with her. But if he comes in disguise, there'll be no danger.
MASTER ANDREA: You're on the right track. But here he is now, the ass — he's on his way out. Take your hat off to him.

Scene xvii.
(MESSER MACO, MASTER ANDREA, *and* ZOPPINO)

ZOPPINO: The lady kisses your hands and feet. She has fallen ill for love of you.
MESSER MACO: Oh, the poor thing! Thank you so much!
ZOPPINO: The lady kissed the letter and the poem a hundred times or more. She has learned it by heart and sings it at the organ.
MESSER MACO: For good news like that I'll order a little marzipan for you next time I send to Siena for some.
MASTER ANDREA: You're too generous! Now Zoppino, let's go inside and work out what Lady Camilla wants Messer Maco to do.

Scene xviii.
(ROSSO, *alone*)

ROSSO: I'm in better shape than I deserve. My master gave me a thousand kisses and calls me Sir. He wants everyone to obey me, even the cellarman. Ha, ha, ha! Oh, yes, yes, yes! I've become a greater master than Marforio.[82] Happy the man who knows how to take advantage of fools. I can see it now — everyone will tip their hats to me. Now I must find Aloigia and bring her to see him. If this gets out, it'll be too bad for him. But I know every hole in Italy that I can hide in. I have faith in Saint Aloigia. She's got more up her sleeve than the calendar of feast days. I'll probably have to wait an hour or so for her: she's busier than busyness itself.

Scene Scene xix.
(GRILLO, *alone*)

GRILLO: What a babbling simpleton this master of mine is! I tell you, he's such a fool that no one envies him. But he's in good hands now — Master Andrea and Zoppino. The one would swindle usury itself, and the other is so learned he'd drive the Sapienzia Capranica[83] to the madhouse. Well, there's no limit to what nature can do — he'd even believe that donkeys can teach school. As good old Strascino[84] used to say, he's a noodle without salt, cheese, or fire.

Scene xx.
(MASTER ANDREA, ZOPPINO, *and* MESSER MACO)

MESSER MACO: She loves me, does she?
MASTER ANDREA: More than if she'd given birth to you.
MESSER MACO: If the little rascal has a child by me, I'll pay for the cradle — the little sweetheart, the good-for-nothing, the scamp.
ZOPPINO: Let's get back to business. I think the surest thing would be for him to come dressed as a porter, with Grillo following him, dressed in his clothes.
MESSER MACO: Dress me up properly, Master.

MASTER ANDREA: Don't worry. But you'll have to learn a few words to disguise your speech. If someone asks you if you're a porter, say *oida*.

MESSER MACO: *Ola.*

MASTER ANDREA: Fine. And if someone asks, "Are you from Bergamo?" say *maide, maide.*

MESSER MACO: *Be, be.*

MASTER ANDREA: And if someone says, "When did you come here, porter?" answer *anco.*

MESSER MACO: *Cacaro.*

MASTER ANDREA: Ha, ha, ha! Excellent! Go along with Grillo to disguise yourself. Your clothes are inside.

Scene xxi.
(MASTER ANDREA *and* ZOPPINO)

ZOPPINO: Let's put a load on him that'll break his back.

MASTER ANDREA: No, that would be too much. It'll be enough to dress him as a porter, and the moment he's at his place by the door, just change your cloak and ask him if he wants to carry someone to the hospital who's sick with the plague.

ZOPPINO: I get it. I'll give you a good laugh. A prank like this would make the Old Testament young again. I'll see you later.

Scene xxii.
(GRILLO, *dressed as* MESSER MACO, *and* MASTER ANDREA)

GRILLO: Do I look like a gentleman?

MASTER ANDREA: Don't ruin the joke. We want him to believe that he really is the Sicilian porter — then take him you-know-where.

Scene xxiii.
(MESSER MACO, MASTER ANDREA, *and* GRILLO)

MASTER ANDREA: The spirit of wisdom itself wouldn't recognize you. But now's the time to show us how smart you are. Sit yourself down by the lady's door, and if anyone goes by pretend that you're here to carry a trunk. But if you see that there's no one in the street, go inside the house and do you-know-what with her.

MESSER MACO: But gently, I swear to God. I kiss your hand.

MASTER ANDREA: Now you go ahead — we'll be right behind you. If you have the bad luck to come across that cheating Spaniard, Grillo, who looks just like you when he's wearing your clothes, well, walk right past him — he won't suspect a thing with you dressed like that. Do you understand, lunkhead?

MESSER MACO: I've got it. But walk close behind; someone might steal me from myself.

Scene xxiv.
(MASTER ANDREA and GRILLO)

MASTER ANDREA: Here's a story that should be in Boccaccio. Wonderful! He, he, he, ha, ha, ha! The coronation of the Abbot of Gaeta[85] was nothing to this, even though they had him riding on an elephant. Of all the tricks they played in the palace in the old days there wasn't one as good as this one.

GRILLO: Is this Zoppino ever a rascal! What a clever old buzzard! Look how he pretends to be someone else, while Messer Mescolone[86] there sits himself down and stays there as solid as a house.

MASTER ANDREA: Let's go closer and listen to what old Zoppino is telling him.

Scene xxv.
(MESSER MACO, dressed as a porter, and ZOPPINO)

ZOPPINO: Do you have a partner to help you carry an invalid to Santo Spirito?[87]

MESSER MACO: Spirit? You know very well I have spirit!

ZOPPINO: Santo Spirito, I said. It's only the plague.

MESSER MACO: The plague? No, I don't have it.

ZOPPINO: It's no joking matter, you fool! Is bread so cheap that you don't need any work?

MESSER MACO: If bread is cheap, tough luck for you.

Scene xxvi.
(MASTER ANDREA, MESSER MACO, GRILLO, *and* ZOPPINO)

MASTER ANDREA: Hey Sicilian, do this gentleman a favor. It's an errand of mercy.

MESSER MACO: Master Andrea, are you joking, or have these clothes turned me into somebody else?

MASTER ANDREA: You talk like a Sienese, and every Christmas the Sienese embroider their cloaks just like that. What a rascal!

MESSER MACO: Isn't this me, then?

MASTER ANDREA: To the gallows with you!

GRILLO: Maybe you'll find what you're looking for there, you damned bastard you.

MESSER MACO: For God's sake, Grillo, you thief — you're making fun of me. Give me back my clothes, you cheating swindler, you!

MASTER ANDREA: Stand back, you boor, you coward, or I'll kill you!

MESSER MACO: Oh dear, dear, I'm in trouble.

ZOPPINO: Someone who just passed by said the Governor has put out a proclamation that anyone who knows about, or has seen, or is hiding a certain Messer Maco from Siena must report him, or his life will be forfeit, because he came to Rome without a passport.

GRILLO: Oh no! I'm done for!

MASTER ANDREA: Don't worry — take those clothes off and we'll put them on this porter. You put on his cloak. When the police find him they'll hang him in your place.

MESSER MACO: Hang me? Mercy! Run! Run! Help me! I'm a dead man!

ZOPPINO: Hold him, hold him! Take this! And that! Spy! Thief! Ha, ha, ha, ha!

MASTER ANDREA: Run after him, Grillo, and bring him back home. Tell him we played a trick on him — to amuse the lady. Tricks like this are all the rage in Rome. He's from a good family and some of his relatives may not think it's funny, and that would be bad for us.

GRILLO: I'll go. He looks as silly as an owl in a crowd of Florentine bankers. There are guys with the gift of the gab who get fat making up tricks like this, the way others get rich from money-lending.

Act III

Scene i.
(PARABOLANO *and his steward,* VALERIO)

PARABOLANO: Good, clever, discreet, and well behaved: that's Rosso! No question about it!

VALERIO: The way you praise Rosso you'd think he's the one who put you where you are.

PARABOLANO: He doesn't come to me with the servants' complaints.

VALERIO: That's because he's a liar.

PARABOLANO: Or tells me the footmen haven't been paid.

VALERIO: Because he doesn't care what happens to you.

PARABOLANO: Or that the colt's having a fit.

VALERIO: And so you believe his lies?

PARABOLANO: Or that the merchant's dunning us for the fabric.

VALERIO: But you've got to pay your debts.

PARABOLANO: He may not have brought me verses singing my praises; what he has brought me is life, and health, and peace. I consider him a true friend, the best of companions, a blood brother.

VALERIO: Well I'm amazed that you don't like those clever fellows who travel from court to court.

PARABOLANO: Look, I don't live on poetry. And in a couple of days I'll have got rid of all those philosophers who've been hanging around the house. I've been keeping them in food and drink against my better judgment. I want to share everything I have with Rosso. He has plucked me out of hell and placed me in paradise; he has given me life; he has revived my parched, dried-up hopes for the passions of love. And now off you go — I'm expecting Rosso and the welcome news that only he can bring.

Scene ii.
(ROSSO *and* ALOIGIA)

ROSSO: I leave it to you.
ALOIGIA: You think this is the first time I've done this?
ROSSO: No, no.
ALOIGIA: Then leave it to me. This must be your master now.
ROSSO: That's him.
ALOIGIA: I could tell it was him — the way he cracks his knuckles, and raises his face to the sky, and puts his finger to his mouth or his hand to his cheek — those are the signs of love. Oh, what fools these gentlemen are! They'll be pining away for a princess, but then some slut comes along and their appetite is satisfied. I've seen them, even in the Dietro Banchi![88] And then they boast how they said or did something with lady such-and-such, or something else with madame so-and-so.
ROSSO: I believe it! It must be quite a chore, managing an affair with a great lady.
ALOIGIA: That's for sure. The only ones who can bring it off are either servants or stewards, and that's only because it's so convenient for them.
ROSSO: Boy, am I happy to have all those worries about women behind me. It amazes me the way those loafers chase after them — at vespers, or mass, or during Lent; cold or hot, night or day. If they happen to reach their goal — after twenty years of trying — then, after a thousand false starts and a four-hour wait in some dirty, dangerous hole or other, a little cough or a sneeze will ruin everything, and bring disgrace on the lady and her whole family. But let's talk about our Orlando.[89] Step aside a little and I'll do what I have to with the Master.

Scene iii.
(ROSSO, PARABOLANO, *and* ALOIGIA)

PARABOLANO: Welcome, dearest Rosso.
ROSSO: This is the nurse of that . . . that . . . You know what I mean.
PARABOLANO: You're the one who has the angel in her care?
ALOIGIA: I am Your Lordship's servant, and my Laura sends her respects.

PARABOLANO: I kneel to await her message.
ALOIGIA: I'm the one who should be kneeling, speaking to such a great gentleman.
PARABOLANO: Come on, get up—enough of this Spanish nonsense!
ALOIGIA: My lady kisses your hand. She has no other god but you. But I'm ashamed to come to you dressed in such a shabby gown. Forgive me.
PARABOLANO: This gold chain will buy you a new one. Take it.
ALOIGIA: Thank you so much! You didn't need to, really!
ROSSO: Didn't I tell you? He's gives away a hundred ducats as carelessly as a merchant steals them. [*aside*] I'm lying in my teeth.
ALOIGIA: I can believe it.
ROSSO: He gives us more clothes every year than they sell in the Piazza Navona.[90] [*aside*] If only the bastard would pay us our salaries! [*aloud*] I won't mention food and drink, but in the servants' mess it's always carnival time. [*aside*] More like it's always Lent—we're all skinnier than a fast.
ALOIGIA: I am your slave.
ROSSO: And friendly with his servants? Why, we're all his pals. [*aside*] I wish his life was as short as one of his friendly looks.
ALOIGIA: It's a gentleman's duty.
ROSSO: Would he use his influence to help us out if we needed it? Why, for the least of his servants he'd speak to the Pope himself! [*aside*] He should live so long! He wouldn't lift a finger—not if he saw us with the rope around our necks.
PARABOLANO: It's only to be of use to my friends that I am what I am, and Rosso knows it. But please, describe Laura's face when you told her about me.
ALOIGIA: The face of an empress!
PARABOLANO: What does she say about me? How does she say it?
ALOIGIA: She speaks with great respect; she's like sugar and honey.
PARABOLANO: What promises does she make to me, her servant?
ALOIGIA: Great ones! Magnificent ones!
PARABOLANO: Do you think she's pretending?
ALOIGIA [*ironically*]: Pretending? Oh sure!
PARABOLANO: How do you know?

ALOIGIA: Why, she's fallen ill on account of you. Besides, she's a noblewoman.
PARABOLANO: Does she love anyone else?
ALOIGIA: No sir.
PARABOLANO: Are you sure?
ALOIGIA: I'm certain.
PARABOLANO: What is she doing now?
ROSSO: [*aside*]: She's taking a piss.
ALOIGIA: She's cursing the day, because it never seems to end.
PARABOLANO: What does the day matter, so long as heaven's at the end of it?
ALOIGIA: It will feel like a thousand years before she's with you tonight.
PARABOLANO: Reverend Mother, let me have a few words with you in private.
ALOIGIA: Whatever Your Lordship pleases.
PARABOLANO: Wait here, Rosso, we'll be back in a moment.
ROSSO: I'll stay, but I'm not happy about it.

Scene iv.
(MESSER MACO *and* ROSSO)

MESSER MACO: What should I do?
ROSSO: Hang yourself.
MESSER MACO: The police are looking for me. There must be some mistake.
ROSSO: Well your face doesn't exactly inspire trust.
MESSER MACO: Do you know Messer Rapolano?[91]
ROSSO: Messer Maco, what's that you're wearing? Have you gone mad?
MESSER MACO: Well, Master Andrea was taking me to the whores, and . . .

Scene v.
(PARABOLANO, ALOIGIA, MESSER MACO, *and* ROSSO)

PARABOLANO: What are you saying, Rosso?
ROSSO: Well as you can see, that rascal Master Andrea has talked your friend Messer Maco here into wearing these clothes.
PARABOLANO: You are Messer Maco?

MESSER MACO: Yes, I am, I am!
PARABOLANO: Rosso, you go along with dear old Mother here. And you, Messer Maco, come into the house with me. What a scoundrel that blockhead Master Andrea is! I don't know if I can ever forgive him!
MESSER MACO: Don't mind my teacher. He's just playing a trick on me.

Scene vi.
(ALOIGIA *and* ROSSO)

ROSSO: What did he tell you?
ALOIGIA: That he's on the point of death. Listen, I've screwed in every whorehouse in Italy. In my heyday neither Lorenzina nor Beatrice could have kept up with me. I had minks and sables; I had parrots, monkeys — everything! You understand?
ROSSO: And I've been servant to an innkeeper, monk, tax-collector, go-between, stool-pigeon, cop, hangman, coachman, miller, singer, jailbird, and con-man. That's my story. Make what you want of it.
ALOIGIA: Look, I meant no offence — all I meant to say is that of all the things I've done, nothing has given me more trouble than this one. Listen, I have a few years up my ass. I used to be a lady, but I had to start from the bottom again, renting rooms, washing clothes, cooking, selling candles.
ROSSO: Look, Aloigia, you should be glad I put this affair in your hands. It may be your last one. They're using fewer and fewer women at court. You know why? Well, they can't take a wife, so they take a husband instead; they satisfy their appetites much better that way, without breaking the law.
ALOIGIA: God save us! What a pack of wild animals that court is! And I'm talking right up as far as the bishops who wear the mitres! And they don't even seem ashamed of it!
ROSSO: Those are wise words, by God. Your confessor should use you in a sermon.
ALOIGIA: You're right. But I'm not looking for worldly success. I learned from my old mentor that before you ride in a fine coach you've got to ride a donkey. A beautifully decorated cardinal's

mitre wouldn't be worthwhile if the neighbors claimed it was all done just for the glory of it. But while we've been talking I've thought of a way to give Parabolano what he wants and at the same time to keep ourselves out of trouble, now that we've gone this far.

ROSSO: Tell me! Tell me!

ALOIGIA: Ercolano the baker has a wife who's really something. I'll see to it that she's with your master tonight, in my house. When gentlemen want something it's like a fever. And they always pick the worst of us women. He'll never catch on.

ROSSO: Let me give you a kiss! Never give up, you crown of all queens! Boy, if you hadn't found a way out I could see myself getting into quite a fix! Now my dumb master will get himself the flower of Rome, and as far as we're concerned, *salvum me fac.*[*] It's clear as can be! Well, it's agreed, then. I'll see you later.

Scene vii.
(FLAMINIO *and* VALERIO)

VALERIO: In these last few minutes you've gone crazy. If you take my advice you'll stay in service!

FLAMINIO: I've definitely decided to find a new master. As the Spaniard said, it's better to lose than to lose a lot. Boy oh boy! When I think of it: fifteen years I've served him! He never ate or mounted a horse without my looking after him. And now I have nothing. I feel like drowning myself. And I'm not so stupid that if some benefit had been thrown my way it would've been wasted.

VALERIO: That's the way Fortune works. Sometimes she'll not only get a master to do his servant a good turn, but she'll make a prisoner out of a great King of France[92] for no reason at all.

FLAMINIO: It's true. If the masters wanted to, they could call a halt to their servants' bad luck—just as the nephew of Ancona, the Archbishop of Ravenna, did these past few days. A benefice he gave to the virtuous Master Ubaldino hasn't worked out,

---

[*] 'I hope we get away with it.'

so he borrowed a thousand scudi on interest, gave them to him, and cheated fortune in that way.[93]

VALERIO: There's only one Archbishop of Ravenna, you know.

FLAMINIO: Well I want to get away. I might at least find a master who'd look me in the face maybe once a month, and when I spoke to him his only answer wouldn't be to call me a fool for insisting on doing things my own way. I wouldn't have to pawn my cloak and gown to keep from going hungry. Listen to this, Valerio—yesterday a position worth fifty scudi came vacant. I mentioned it to him right away, but he wouldn't say a word on my behalf. He had them give it to the son of Sibilla the bawd instead.

VALERIO: Masters do as they please. They advance whoever they want, and they ruin whoever they want. It's a question of devoting yourself to the good goddess Fortune, and make the best of what you've got. Here it is in a nutshell—one person will serve forever and never have anything to show for it, while somebody else, the first day he's in service he'll be rich. But you mustn't give up hope—a courtier's stock rises the moment he least expects it.

FLAMINIO: Maybe so, but some people are so unlucky that the moment never comes. Do you think he wasn't full of promises when I first came to work for him? A person who tosses words around like that should be prepared to do something as well. I'm finding a new master.

VALERIO: Where will you go? It's a mess everywhere. If you go to Milan, God only knows how the Duke will end up. In Ferrara the prince does nothing but keep open house. There are no more kings in Naples. In Urbino the Duke is nervous, because past difficulties are still giving him trouble.[94] Believe me, when the court of Rome suffers, everyone else suffers as well.

FLAMINIO: I'll go to Mantua. His Excellency the Marquis Federico[95] sees that everyone gets the bread he needs. I'll stay there until Our Lord the Pope straightens out the world—and I'm not just talking about Italy. That's when I'll come back, because I'm sure that His Holiness will put virtue back where it belongs, just as his brother Leo did.[96]

VALERIO: You talk it over with me again soon, then do it my way and you'll be fine. Flatter the Master; when he's got a woman or a boy in his bedroom, say he's reciting his offices. All they want is for you to praise everything they do, both the good and the bad. You know what you can say and still live like a free man. The only thing that offends or displeases them is the truth.

FLAMINIO: But don't you see, Valerio, it's always the evildoers who are rewarded. I'll see you again, but I'll do what's best for myself. Envy's everywhere at court—along the corridors, in the chambers, up and down the staircases—but no one has ever had reason to be envious of me. You can see what a wretched state I'm in. But I don't mind, because no courtier's soul will ever be damned because of me.

VALERIO: Some might think you're envious, since you say your master rewards those who don't deserve it.

FLAMINIO: I didn't say that out of envy, but because I was disgusted at how little sense he has.

VALERIO: Goodbye.

Scene viii.
(PARABOLANO and ROSSO)

PARABOLANO: It's a sweet thing indeed to love and be loved.

ROSSO: The sweetest things are eating and drinking.

PARABOLANO: Sweet will be my Laura.

ROSSO: If anyone wants her. As for me, I'd prefer a pitcher of Greek wine to Angela the Greek. I'd rather have a meal than Amelia.[97] If gluttony could get you into paradise, I'd be at the head table by now.

PARABOLANO: The ambrosia that drops from the mouths of lovers has a sweetness very different from the taste of partridge and Greek wine.

ROSSO: I've tasted hundreds of them. I've tasted Lorenzina, and Lady Momma-Doesn't-Want-Me-To,[98] and others, too, some of the most popular ones, but the only thing I found there was guck that'd turn the stomach of a galley slave.

PARABOLANO: Don't compare cranes and partridges. Have some respect for the ladies.

ROSSO: Why? Don't they piss like peasants?

PARABOLANO: I'm a fool to talk to you.

ROSSO: And I'm a fool to answer you. Tell me, Master, isn't there one thing sweeter than the ambrosia you're talking about? What about the honey that drops from tongues that can speak both the good and the evil? Ah! Now I've got you.

PARABOLANO: Ha, ha, ha!

ROSSO: Oh, those verses that Master Pasquino writes — they're marvellous! The barber says they should read one every day between the epistle and the gospel. Christ, they'd bring a blush to the cheeks of shame itself.

PARABOLANO: You seem very familiar with the poets.

ROSSO: I used to work for Messer Antonio Lelio,[99] and I know a thousand fine phrases by heart.

PARABOLANO: Come on, we must talk about Aloigia. Let's go inside.

Scene ix.
(MESSER MACO and MASTER ANDREA)

MESSER MACO: Master Andrea, how do we come into this world?

MASTER ANDREA: Through a very wide window.

MESSER MACO: And why do we come into this world?

MASTER ANDREA: To live.

MESSER MACO: How do we live, then?

MASTER ANDREA: By eating and drinking.

MESSER MACO: I eat like a wolf and drink like a horse, so I guess I'll live forever. Well, when a man has done living, what does he do then?

MASTER ANDREA: He dies in a hole like a spider. But let's get back to Gian Manenti.[100]

MESSER MACO: Who was this Gian Manenti?

MASTER ANDREA: A great courtier and musician who made a new man of himself in those same molds where we're going to re-make you.

MESSER MACO: How do they work?

MASTER ANDREA: You'll have to soak in lukewarm water.

MESSER MACO: Will it hurt?

MASTER ANDREA: Look, when they make cannons, and bells, and towers, do they hurt?

MESSER MACO: I don't think so. But I thought that cannons and bells and towers grew like pine trees.
MASTER ANDREA: You were way off the mark.
MESSER MACO: Will I turn out well?
MASTER ANDREA: Tremendously well. It's easier to make a man than a cannon.
MESSER MACO: It is, eh?
MASTER ANDREA: Yes sir. Now we must arrange for the doctor and the molds and the medicines.

Scene x.
(GRILLO, *the servant*, MESSER MACO, *and* MASTER ANDREA)

GRILLO: Until Signor Parabolano sent word that Your Lordship had been found, we were desperate—the lady had people looking for you everywhere.
MESSER MACO: The poor thing was worried about me, was she?
MASTER ANDREA: Grillo, listen carefully to what I tell you. I want my lord here to be made over, like the other courtiers.
GRILLO: You've made a good start—soon you'll be in velvet. But for the love of God you'd better warn the ladies so that they can get a good supply of mattresses—when you've become a courtier they'll throw themselves out of the windows for love of you, and you don't want them to hurt themselves.
MESSER MACO: That would be a shame. I'll see that someone brings mattresses.
GRILLO: What delicacy of feeling!
MASTER ANDREA: Now let's get things moving. Let's go! Quickly!

Scene xi.
(ALOIGIA *and* ROSSO)

ALOIGIA: My heavens, I'm as busy as a marketplace. I've more letters to deliver than a courier, and more messages than an ambassador. Some want ointments for the French disease,[101] others want powders to whiten their teeth or to cure God knows what maladies. And now I bet Rosso's looking for me. What did I tell you?
ROSSO: Drop everything and figure out some way that my master can play with his rod tonight.

ALOIGIA: I've got to say a few words to my confessor, then I'll come and see you.
ROSSO: Hurry up. My master's gone to the palace and he'll be back soon. I'll be around the house.

Scene xii.
(FLAMINIO, *alone*)

FLAMINIO: I'm glad I talked to Valerio. He's a sensible, helpful young fellow, and he wishes me well—although advice is cheap, and what I need right now is help, the way justice needs the help of Pope Clement.[102] I'd be ready to give up hope, but then I compare my fate with that of greater men than myself. That was despicable, the way Cesare[103] was betrayed—he always valued his lord's reputation more than his own life.

Scene xiii.
(VALERIO *and* FLAMINIO)

VALERIO: Who are you talking to, Flaminio?
FLAMINIO: I'm easing my own troubles by talking about someone else's.
VALERIO: Whose troubles do you mean?
FLAMINIO: Cesare's—all Rome's talking about them.
VALERIO: Please, let's talk about something a little more agreeable. What happened to him is too serious. As I've told you, we should respect great men. It's risky as the devil to insult them.
FLAMINIO: The devil indeed! To tell the truth, you risk your life when you tell the truth. But enough of this.
VALERIO: Let's think about your problem. Come to the Banchi with me.[104] I've something to tell you that you're going to like. But let's go inside—I forgot my note of exchange.
FLAMINIO: Let's go—we'll leave by the garden gate.

Scene xiv.
(GRILLO, *alone*)

GRILLO: I've got to find Master Mercurio. He's the best fellow in the world, and the greatest joker. Master Andrea told Messer

Maco that he's the doctor who helps make courtiers. But by God, here he is! Welcome, Master Mercurio.

Scene xv.

(MASTER MERCURIO, *a doctor, and* GRILLO, *servant of* MESSER MACO)

MASTER MERCURIO: What do you want, Grillo?

GRILLO: Master Andrea has the most beautiful prank going on you've ever heard. A Sienese gentleman came to Rome to make himself a cardinal in service to the Pope, and he's taken on Master Andrea as a teacher. Master Andrea's convinced him that the first thing he must do is to take on the shape of a courtier. Now we want to take him to the baths. They're really hard on someone who's never taken one — it's as bad as being seasick. By the time we've shaved him and dressed him, he'll be a laughing stock. You'll be the doctor.

MASTER MERCURIO: Ha, ha, ha! I have an even better idea. You know the hot-water cauldrons?

GRILLO: Yes.

MASTER MERCURIO: We'll put him in there to soak, and we'll tell him that they're the courtiers' molds. But first we'll give him a few pills.

GRILLO: You've got the idea! Let's go to Master Andrea. Messer Priapus is waiting for us.[105]

Scene xvi.

(ALOIGIA *and the* FATHER GUARDIAN *of Araceli*)

ALOIGIA: I was just coming to Araceli[106] to see you, Father, but you've saved me the trouble.

FATHER GUARDIAN: I come to St. Peter's every day to do my devotions.

ALOIGIA: God forgive... I mean God reward you for it. But you're always praying — and you're fatter and handsomer than ever.

FATHER GUARDIAN: I don't follow the rules as strictly as all that — I may not get to paradise today, but there's always tomorrow.

ALOIGIA: True, true, no reason to be in a hurry — and then it's big enough that we'll all fit in, thank God.

FATHER GUARDIAN: That's right. And there'll be room left over, because our souls are like lies — no matter how many millions of them you tell, like Tinca Martelli the Florentine,[107] they don't take up any room. But what miracle made you come to see me?

ALOIGIA: There are two questions I want to clear up. This is the first.

FATHER GUARDIAN: Well?

ALOIGIA: I want to know whether my dear old mentor's soul will go to purgatory.

FATHER GUARDIAN: Purgatory? Yes, for a month or so.

ALOIGIA: They told me it wouldn't.

FATHER GUARDIAN: Don't you think I should know such things?

ALOIGIA: Oh, how wicked of me! I shouldn't have listened to those slanderers. She will go, then?

FATHER GUARDIAN: Yes, take my word for it. What's the other question?

ALOIGIA: Oh, what a memory! I've a mind like a sieve . . . Wait . . . No . . . I've forgotten. Oh, now I remember! The Turk—where is he?

FATHER GUARDIAN: In Calcutta, in Turkey.

ALOIGIA: They're saying in the piazza that in a week's time he'll be in Rome.

FATHER GUARDIAN: So what? Even if he came in four days, what difference would it make?

ALOIGIA: Quite a difference!

FATHER GUARDIAN: But what would happen?

ALOIGIA: It would be terrible—a filthy trick—I can't even think of all that impaling! Impaling! Oooh! But will he come, Father?

FATHER GUARDIAN: No, you silly woman!

ALOIGIA: What a comfort you are to me! Imagine! To impale a poor little woman! May God and your prayers forbid it! I like to have a bit of bread in my mouth, but I could never swallow the Turk!

FATHER GUARDIAN: Now go along, and God bless you. I can't stay with you any longer. I have to hurry. To tell you the truth, I heard in confession that Verucchio's men plan to murder their count, Giovan Maria Giudeo.[108] I'm going to have them arrested, and the first twenty will have their heads cut off. And it'll be all my doing.

ALOIGIA: And a very good thing it is, too. You monks know everything.

FATHER GUARDIAN: That's for certain — no one betrays anyone without our knowing about it. And we know how to get what we want, too — whether it's a bit of veal or a young goat. I'm talking about the priests, of course. As for the minor friars, well, matins, masses, vespers, and compline are for them. They may be bothered in their dreams by a bit of flesh, but they eat with the cats.

ALOIGIA: And I thought you were all saints — you with your sandal-worn feet. Now go along and God bless you. Tomorrow, or whenever you get back, I want you to say San Gregorio's mass for my husband's soul. He may have been a bad man, but come nighttime, I could always do what I wanted with him.

FATHER GUARDIAN: Just come along and you'll be looked after.

Scene xvii.
(ALOIGIA, *alone*)

ALOIGIA: You've got to have certain talents — like the ones my mentor had — if you want to survive. And if you want to know what's going on, you've got to be friends with a monk or two. But let's get back to business. When I think about it, Madonna Maggiorina's death has made me the luckiest woman on earth. When she's in paradise she'll be a good go-between for me up there, just as she always was down here. Now I must go — I don't want Rosso to have to wait all day.

Act IV

Scene i.

(MASTER ANDREA, MESSER MACO, MASTER MERCURIO, *and* GRILLO)

MASTER ANDREA: We have agreed on the price, and Messer Maco is ready to risk taking the medicine.

MESSER MACO: *Tamen,*[*] I'm really wondering about taking pills.

MASTER MERCURIO: *Pillolarum Romane Curie sunt dulciora.*

MESSER MACO: *Nego istud, nego, nego, magister mi.*

MASTER ANDREA: *Hyppograssus affirmat hoc, dico vobis.*

MESSER MACO: *Nego prepositio hanc.*

MASTER MERCURIO: *Domine, usquequo vos non inteligitis glosam de verborum obligatione che sic inquit: totiens quotiens vult diventare cortigianos novissima dies pillole at aque syropus accipere bisognat?*[†]

MESSER MACO: You've used a false rhyme: *bisognat* isn't Tuscan, and I have a Petrarch here in my pocket that'll prove it.[109]

MASTER ANDREA: Come on, now, talk normally, not this gibberish.

MESSER MACO: *Trans fabrilia fabri.*[‡]

MASTER MERCURIO: You know what medlars are, don't you, sir?

MESSER MACO: Yes sir.

---

[*] 'However.'

[†] 'MASTER MERCURIO: The pills of the Roman Curia are sweeter.
MESSER MACO: I deny it, I deny, I deny, my master.
MASTER ANDREA: Hippocrates affirms it, I tell you.
MESSER MACO: I deny that proposition.
MASTER MERCURIO: Sir, now you don't understand the obligation implied in this sentence. Don't you realize that if you want to become a courtier in this day and age you must take pills and syrupy water?'

[‡] 'Through the tools to the work.'

MASTER MERCURIO: Well, in Rome we call medlars "pills," and you can take as many of them as your guts will tolerate.[110]

MASTER ANDREA: Did you understand exactly what Master Mercurio said?

MESSER MACO: Yes, I did. He's a very learned man. I'd eat a thousand medlars for his sake.

MASTER ANDREA: That's the spirit! In Bartolomeo Coglione's time, you'd have been one of Malatesta's best soldiers.[111]

GRILLO: Master, I'd better get going — the molds are waiting.

MESSER MACO: Yes, go ahead, and pick out the best and most comfortable one you can find.

GRILLO: I'll do that. Anything else?

MESSER MACO: Make sure it's big enough to get my whole head in, and see to it that no one's used it before.

MASTER ANDREA: Hurry, Grillo, and check that there's a set of scales. He has to be weighed, because we have to pay a penny a pound the minute he's done. But my dear sir, before you turn into someone else, please swear that you'll be kind to me. You know what usually happens: as soon as you take someone away from tending donkeys, and raise them to the heavens, like Accursio or Serapice,[112] they don't give another thought to their friends or relations.

MESSER MACO: By the body of Judas, I'd like to chuck you under the chin!

MASTER ANDREA: That's a child's oath.

MESSER MACO: By the Gospels!

MASTER ANDREA: That's how a peasant swears.

MESSER MACO: By God's faith!

MASTER ANDREA: The porters say that.

MESSER MACO: By the blessed cross!

MASTER ANDREA: Women's words.

MESSER MACO: Cunt ... Blood ... By the body of ...

MASTER ANDREA: By the body of what?

MESSER MACO: You really want me to swear?

MASTER ANDREA: Why not?

MESSER MACO: Of ... Christ! Of Christ! There! I said it!

MASTER ANDREA: Ah, Messer Maco, I'm joking — you swear like a trooper, and, my dear old fellow, I'm your most devoted servant.

MASTER MERCURIO: Come on, let's not waste time. The molds are getting cold, and here in Rome wood's worth a fortune.

MESSER MACO: Wait, I'll order a load from Siena.

MASTER ANDREA: Ha, ha, ha! Here's the workshop where they make those *plusquam** perfect courtiers — and there's Grillo at the door! How are things, Grillo?

GRILLO: Everything's ready — the molds, the scales, the medlars, and the workmen. The things that you'll see will be more fantastic than the humor of melancholy.

MESSER MACO: Where is the moon right now, Master?

MASTER MERCURIO: What? Oh, a long way off.

MESSER MACO: No, I want to know whether it's full or not.

MASTER MERCURIO: No sir.

MESSER MACO: Good. I was afraid it was, because then *in fluxo ventris* comes, but *sola fides sufficit*. Let's go, *in nomine Domini*.†

Scene ii.
(ALOIGIA *and* ROSSO)

ALOIGIA: Ah, there you are, Rosso. I was asking my confessor when the mid-August feast of the Madonna is, because I've taken a vow to fast the night before. Then I came along the street of *la Piemontese*, and she gave me these sleeves. Then I rinsed my teeth with half a jug of Corsican wine, and now here I am.

ROSSO: To make a long story short, Aloigia, Valerio's got it in for me, and I feel the same way about him. If you were to work out a way we could put him in the boss's bad books, I'd make it worth your while, because then I'd be in charge of things.

ALOIGIA: You give me a cut of your take, and I'll see to it that he breaks his neck on a blade of grass.

ROSSO: It's yours! But tell me how you're going to do it.

ALOIGIA: I'm thinking about that right now.

ROSSO: Work it out carefully — it's important.

ALOIGIA: I've got it! Hold tight!

ROSSO: God, I hope so.

---

*'more than'

†'... the looseness in the belly [comes; but] faith alone suffices; [Let's go], in the name of the Lord.'

ALOIGIA: Here it is.

ROSSO: Well?

ALOIGIA: I'll say Valerio heard us talking about Laura, and he warned her brother, and the brother, whose name is Rienzo di Jacovello,[113] has sworn to make trouble for all of us. But quiet — here's your master.

Scene iii.
(PARABOLANO, ROSSO, *and* ALOIGIA)

PARABOLANO: What is my Soul doing?

ALOIGIA: She's dying for Your Lordship, but . . .

PARABOLANO: "But"? God help me, what do you mean by "but"?

ALOIGIA: It was the act of a scoundrel!

PARABOLANO: What act? Who?

ALOIGIA: You should never do anyone a favor.

ROSSO: That Valerio of yours . . .

PARABOLANO: Valerio? What did Valerio do?

ALOIGIA: He went and told Laura's brother that Rosso and I are pimping for his sister. But don't tell anyone I told you.

PARABOLANO: Is that possible?

ROSSO: I'm ready to explode! I can't keep quiet! The worst man in Rome! He's killed a dozen policemen, and he still goes around armed in spite of the Governor's proclamation. I hope to God you get out of this one in one piece.

PARABOLANO: That traitor! I'll take this dagger and stab him to the heart! That filthy tongue of his!

ALOIGIA: For the love of God, sir, don't get involved in this affair — it'll ruin us!

PARABOLANO: The scoundrel! It serves me right! I dragged him kicking and screaming out of the mud, made a man of him, and now he has an income of a thousand ducats!

ROSSO: That's what I say! I realized he was trying to ruin you, but I held my tongue because Your Lordship would have said I was talking nonsense.

PARABOLANO: Come inside for a while. The pain is tearing me apart!

Scene iv.
(ROSSO, *alone*)

ROSSO: The proverb says, as you make your bed, so must you lie in it; and if you're a donkey but you think you're a deer, you'll lose your patron and you'll never get rich. I've put one over on you, I know it. You'll become the Duke of Tigoli[114] and I hope it kills you, you dressed-up donkey! Now me — I'm a liar, a layabout, a cynic, a cheat, a flatterer, a stool-pigeon, a thief, a perjurer, and a pimp. And that gets you further than being someone like Messer Angelo de Cesis.[115] With Aloigia helping me, I'll bring in fresh merchandise every day, through both the front door and the back. I'll be the favorite — and then it'll be "Up yours, Valerio."

Scene v.
(ALOIGIA *and* ROSSO)

ALOIGIA: I've taken care of him; it only took a couple of words. I promised him that if he comes to my place at eleven he'll find himself with Laura. I told him she'll be all alone in the dark, because she's so shy you couldn't get her there otherwise. We can manage this because her husband's away — he's going to Veletri[116] for the week. But before we arranged all of this he fired Valerio and gave him a good tongue-lashing. Now away with you — I've no time to waste.

ROSSO: What a witch she is! If the pupil can set things up so easily, think what the teacher must have been like! What did you say, sir?

Scene vi.
(PARABOLANO *and* ROSSO)

PARABOLANO: Is that the way Valerio talked about me?
ROSSO: There's more I could tell you, but I don't like telling tales.
PARABOLANO: I'll have him locked up!
ROSSO: You ought to do that — you've no worse enemy than him. I don't know what poison it was that he bought . . . But I shouldn't . . .
PARABOLANO: Are you sure?

ROSSO: I know what I'm talking about. Nobody can stand him — not even the street kids, or the whores, or the gamblers.

PARABOLANO: Tomorrow morning I'll hand him over to the law.

ROSSO: He talks about your mother, and your sisters, and your family, and he doesn't care what he says about them. Now I don't like fighting, otherwise a couple of days ago I'd have shown him a thing or two about gossiping about your affairs.

PARABOLANO: There you go — that's what happens when you trust a servant. Dear, dear, dear! Take the keys, Rosso, all of them, and use them properly.

ROSSO: I'm no expert, but at least I'll be faithful to you. As far as other things are concerned, I've no reason to envy anyone — and I'm not just bragging. But let's get this little annoyance out of the way, and if he's done something wrong, let's punish him. Tonight Aloigia will do what she's promised, and I'll be left with my tongue hanging out. What's the first thing you're going to say to her?

PARABOLANO: What would you say?

ROSSO: I'd let my hands do the talking. But it's too bad she can't see your face. There's not a woman in Rome who doesn't pine away whenever you pass by. I'm not just flattering you — it's the truth! And if I were a woman, I'd want you to do a job on me right away, without wasting time. If you'd like to take a ride to kill some time until evening, the little mule is ready.

PARABOLANO: I think I'll walk. Let's go this way. There's nothing I'd rather do than talk to you.

ROSSO: This is your slave you're talking to, Master, and I'm as reliable as death itself. When I think about your Lady Laura, I'm struck dumb by her beauty. She's elegant, she's charming, and yet she's grave and demure and virtuous. Jesus, she was made for you!

Scene vii.
(VALERIO *and* FLAMINIO)

VALERIO: My master's love has completely turned against me. He fired me. It was as if I'd murdered his father or something. Why is it that gentlemen are so easily taken in by the worst kind of people? By God, I've stumbled right into what I've always been afraid of. It's true that I have enough to live comfortably, like a gentleman, and I wouldn't mind taking a rest and never have to serve again. But I don't like to leave my master under a cloud — people will think I did something wrong. So you see, Flaminio, everyone has his troubles.

FLAMINIO: "Oppressed by ills, I fear the worst," as Petrarch said.[117] I was hoping you might be able to do something for me, but now I see you've had worse luck than I have. They say that misery loves company, but I swear, Valerio, my love for you makes me feel even worse.

VALERIO: I want to find out if this is a case of infatuation. I'm sure he is in love. And I wonder if the whole thing was invented by that rogue Rosso. He's been talking in secret with him all the time lately. But that's the way the world goes.

FLAMINIO: Don't rush into things. You've always acted wisely: use your wisdom now, when your honor and the fruits of so many years' service are at stake.

VALERIO: Goodbye. I'll be able tell you soon where this thing came from.

Scene viii.

(TOGNA, *wife of* ERCOLANO *the baker, and* ALOIGIA)

[ALOIGIA *knocks*]

TOGNA: Who's there?

ALOIGIA: It's Aloigia, dear.

TOGNA: Wait, I'll come right down.

ALOIGIA: Good day, my love.

TOGNA: What do you want, Granny?

ALOIGIA: Come to my house at ten o'clock tonight. There's something I want you to do for me, in confidence — it'll be to your advantage.

TOGNA: Oh no, that's just my luck. My husband's got so jealous I don't know where I am any more. But...

ALOIGIA: What do you mean, "but..."? Your luck? You do as I tell you, and don't be so childish.

TOGNA: When it comes right down to it, I suppose I can't pass this one up. I'll be there if it kills me. It'll serve him right, the drunken swine.

ALOIGIA: Thank you. Oh, by the way, come dressed as a man. Some crazy things happen in Rome at night—you could be gang-raped,[118] *verbi gratia.*[*] And remember, thanks to me you're half-way there.

TOGNA: Thanks a million. Fine, then, I'll come. And as for Ercolano, to hell with him.

Scene ix.

(ERCOLANO *the baker,* TOGNA, *his wife, and* ALOIGIA)

ERCOLANO: What's all the jabbering about?
ALOIGIA: About your soul.
ERCOLANO: How pious of you!
TOGNA: You should be thankful.
ERCOLANO: Shut up, bitch!
TOGNA: Can't a person have a talk with a nice old lady?
ERCOLANO: Where's my shovel . . .
ALOIGIA: My good man, Antonia was just asking me when the Lenten service at San Lorenzo Extra Muros[119] will be.
ERCOLANO: There's nothing in that for me. Now get the hell out, and don't let me see you around here again. And you—in the house! By . . .
TOGNA: Go to hell!

Scene x.

(ERCOLANO, *alone*)

ERCOLANO: If you keep goats, you'll have horns. This little wench of mine isn't up to standard. I've noticed how she goes out at night to amuse herself. I'm not so blind drunk I can't see I'm from Corneto, and now with this Aloigia hanging around there's no room for doubt. When I get back home I'm going to play drunk, then I'll know for sure whether I've come straight from Cervia.[120]

---

[*] 'as they say'

Scene xi.
(ERCOLANO *and* TOGNA)

ERCOLANO: Come down here, you lazy loafer! Togna! Who do you think I'm talking to?

TOGNA: What do you want?

ERCOLANO: Don't expect me for supper.

TOGNA: So what else is new?

ERCOLANO: Now you listen to me . . .

TOGNA: You'd do better to stay home, instead of hanging around taverns and running after whores.

ERCOLANO: Get off my back. Get my bed made right now, so I can sleep as soon as I get in.

TOGNA: I always have to eat with the cat. I know the devil didn't want you to join up with someone who'd treat you the way you deserve, but I'm far too good for you.

ERCOLANO: Don't perch up there in the window, showing yourself off like some slut.

TOGNA: The wolves will eat me up.

ERCOLANO: That's enough. You know what I'm talking about. I'm going.

TOGNA: To hell! But enough talk—it's time to do something. If two mouths kiss, one of them's bound to stink. Yours with wine and mine with love. I'll see that you wear them, even if you burst for it, you jealous drunkard!

Scene xii.
(PARABOLANO *and* ROSSO)

PARABOLANO: Who knows? Perhaps the sun and the moon are in love with her!

ROSSO: That may very well be, because the sun and the moon are as horny as can be.

PARABOLANO: It frightens me when I think of it: the house she lives in, the clothes she wears, the bed that keeps her warm, the water that washes her, and the flowers that she smells—all these can claim her love.

ROSSO: You're too fearful. May Cupid take heaven and earth by the hair.

PARABOLANO: I hope to God I'm wrong. Now let's go back home.

Scene xiii.
(GRILLO, *alone*)

GRILLO: Ha, ha, ha! Please, no more laughing—stop!—let me speak. Ha, ha, ha!—please! Messer Maco—ha, ha!—Messer Maco was in the molds. He threw up till you'd think his soul would come next. They shaved him, dressed him in new clothes, perfumed him, and talked a whole pile of nonsense. Now he's saying things that'd bring a laugh to a melancholic. He wants all Rome for himself, the ladies, and the power, and the glory. That crazy Master Andrea makes him believe things that would make a liar out of the Gospels. Messer says *mi-mi-mi* and *si-si-si* just like a Bergamese, and uses words that not even an interpreter could understand. If I wanted to tell you exactly what he says I'd have to have the memory of a Ricordo.[121] But enough of that. He sent me to look for marzipan, the Sienese kind. But I've got something more interesting to do—let him wait till the crow comes home.[122] Oh, I forgot—Master Andrea has a mirror; it's concave, and it shows people looking the opposite of what they really are. When they come out of the bath he makes them look into it, and they lose all hope. You stay here and watch for him. As for me, I've seen enough.

Scene xiv.
(ROSSO, *alone*)

ROSSO: Damn him! What did I tell you? Christ! No sooner do I sit down to have a drink but I have to run for Aloigia. I've become his messenger boy, lovesick as he is. Well, as long as he promises to make me chamberlain . . . And yet I'd rather be a nobody than a chamberlain. Do you know anyone who loves them? There's one I know who lends money at high interest to his own master—and it's the same money he's stolen from him! You know, all the stuff they give to their whores is like so many mouthfuls stolen from their hungry servants. By God's asshole, if it weren't for the example of Pope Clement's majordomo—the one exception to the rule—I'd spill the beans. But where did Aloigia go, the old witch?

Scene xv.
(ROMANELLO, *a Jew, and* ROSSO)

ROMANELLO: Any old iron! Any old iron!
ROSSO: I think I'll play one on this Jew just like I did on the fishmonger.
ROMANELLO: Any old iron! Any old iron!
ROSSO: Come here, Jew. What do you want for this monk's gown?
ROMANELLO: Try it on. If it fits we can make a deal.
ROSSO: Help me with it. I'd like to get out of these rags for once.
ROMANELLO: It's just right! Like it was made for you!
ROSSO: How much?
ROMANELLO: Ten ducats.
ROSSO: That's too high.
ROMANELLO: What'll you give me?
ROSSO: Eight scudi. And I'll take this cape for one of my monks at Araceli as well.
ROMANELLO: I'm happy you're buying it for your brother. I'll try it on myself so you can see if it's big enough.
ROSSO: I wouldn't mind seeing how it looks on you.
ROMANELLO: Give me a hand. Here, hand me the cord and the scapular. What do you think?
ROSSO: I like it. It's good material, and it's almost new.
ROMANELLO: Very new. It belonged to Cardinal Araceli *in minoribus*.[123]
ROSSO: Turn around so I can see how it drapes.
ROMANELLO: There.
ROSSO [*fleeing with the gown, with the Jew after him dressed as a friar*]: Thief! Thief! Stop him! Catch him! Thief! Thief!

Scene xvi.
(POLICEMAN, ROSSO, *and* ROMANELLO)

POLICEMAN: Stop in the name of the law! What's going on here?
ROSSO: This monk came out of a tavern and started running after me like a crazy man. I didn't want to argue with a priest, so I took off.
ROMANELLO: Officer, this guy's swindled me, sir. I'm Romanello the Jew, who . . .

POLICEMAN: Sacrilege! You scoundrel! Making fun of Christians going around wearing holy robes! Take him to jail.

ROMANELLO: Is this what you call justice?

ROSSO: Captain, Your Lordship had better do something about this, because I'm with someone who'd make you sorry you didn't. This kind of thing shouldn't happen to a person who's just going about his business.

POLICEMAN: Don't worry, he'll pay for it. A few strokes of the lash should get the wine out of his head.

Scene xvii.
(ROSSO, *alone*)

ROSSO: Armelino's in charge of this district,[124] and if he doesn't keep this guy on the job for ten more years he'll be making a big mistake. He's got a great eye for a thief, hasn't he! Oh, the crooked things that go on here in this filthy Rome of ours! God must be truly patient, or he'd have sent down some great calamity by now. I deserve to be hung up like a piece of antipasto, and he's let me go free, while poor Romanello's lost his robe and they've sent him to prison. It'll cost him more than just a few fast words to get out of this one. You need good luck to get along in the world. Now that I feel better, let's find the old lady.

Scene xviii.
(MASTER MERCURIO, MASTER ANDREA, *and* MESSER MACO)

MASTER ANDREA: It must be a hundred years at least since anyone's seen as handsome a fellow as you!

MASTER MERCURIO: By God, you should be thankful for the high quality glue they use in those molds!

MESSER MACO: Ha, ha! Show me the mirror. I feel like a new man! Oh, the pain I suffered! But now I'm a courtier and I feel fine. Here, give me the mirror. Oh, my God! I'm ruined! Maimed! Done for! Oh, my mouth! My nose! Merciful heavens! *Vita dulcedo . . . et verbum caro factum est.**

MASTER MERCURIO: What's wrong? Does your body hurt?

---

*'life sweetness . . . and the word became flesh.'

MESSER MACO: I'm finished! I'm not myself! . . . *regnum tuum . . . panem nostrum . . .** Swindlers! You've changed the way I look! I'll have you charged as thieves! Thieves! . . . *visibilium et invisibilium . . .*†

MASTER ANDREA: It never hurts to do a little praying, but do you have to throw yourself on the ground? Stand up and take a good look in the mirror.

MESSER MACO: Scoundrels! Give me my face, and you can take yours back. If I recover, I solemnly swear I'll say the pestilential psalms for a month.

MASTER ANDREA: Fine, fine! But look at yourself in the mirror again.

MESSER MACO: I won't.

MASTER ANDREA: Yes you will.

MESSER MACO: *Laudati pueri dominum!*‡ I've recovered! I'm back together again! And handsomer than ever!

> Oh little star of love! Oh angel's courtier!
> Oh carven image! Visage oriental! . . .

MASTER MERCURIO: You do your celebrating to music? My, what a voice!

MESSER MACO: I want all the ladies of the court—right now. I want to be Pope and I want to screw Camilla. Now! Now! Let's get moving. I'm in a hurry!

MASTER ANDREA: Away you go, Master Mercurio. See the cashier at the Chisi[125] tomorrow, and you'll be paid on Messer Maco's behalf.

MASTER MERCURIO: I'll do that—and, Your Lordship, I kiss your hands.

Scene xix.
(MASTER ANDREA *and* MESSER MACO)

MESSER MACO: I want to screw the lady, I tell you, screw her! Let's go!

---

*'. . . your kingdom . . . our bread . . .'
†'visible and invisible'
‡'Praise the Lord, children.'

MASTER ANDREA: Don't you want to wear something more suitable?

MESSER MACO: Shittable? What are you talking about? The lady, I said! The lady!

MASTER ANDREA: Take it easy! Let's go inside and we'll get your sword and your cape, and then we'll go to the lady. You don't go around Rome at night in a bathrobe.

MESSER MACO: Let's go. The devil's got into me!

Scene xx.
(ALOIGIA *and* ROSSO)

ROSSO [*knocks*]: Aloigia?

ALOIGIA: I was just looking for you. There's something I want to tell you.

ROSSO: What? Isn't everything ready?

ALOIGIA: Togna, Ercolano's...

ROSSO: What? She doesn't want to come?

ALOIGIA: I was talking to her a while ago, and her husband caught us.

ROSSO: And did he realize that...

ALOIGIA: Don't worry. Go tell your master to get ready. At eleven o'clock he has to break a couple of lances. Make sure he understands what he has to do. My compliments to His Excellency. Goodbye.

ROSSO: Goodbye. I'll go this way so I don't meet my master. Too late — here he is.

Scene xxi.
(PARABOLANO *and* ROSSO)

PARABOLANO: Well? What's happening?

ROSSO: To make a long story short, your friend will come at eleven o'clock. So you'd better take a dose of something to build up your strength.

PARABOLANO: She's a fine woman, that Aloigia!

ROSSO: The most loving woman in the world.

PARABOLANO: I'll be worn out by eleven. Can you hear them sounding, Rosso? Listen: one... two...

ROSSO: Sure, it's the church bells calling to prayer.

PARABOLANO: Oh! Right. What will we do while we're waiting?
ROSSO: A little snack.
PARABOLANO: What an idea!
ROSSO: Well I don't want to eat like some monk of the Papal Seal, you know.
PARABOLANO: For pity's sake, let's talk about Laura.
ROSSO: For pity's sake, let's pick up a quick bite to eat and a couple of glasses of wine on the run.
PARABOLANO: I feed myself with the memory of my lady. I crave nothing else to satisfy my hunger. But I want to make you happy. Let's go.
ROSSO: *Gratis vobis.*[*] You'd soon forget your memories if you were hungry.

---

[*] 'I thank you.'

Act V

Scene i.
(*Valerio, alone*)

VALERIO: No question about it now, my master's angry with me. I can see it on the face of every servant. Oh, oh, oh, oh! It's really true: you never see a face at court that's not a sham. Up till now they treated me almost as if I were the master. Everyone praised my wisdom, my goodness, my generosity. Everyone loved me. Now nobody knows me, and everyone's having his say about me. And it's the ones I've always encouraged and helped out with my own money who are the first to insult me. Well, there we are! The very walls of the rooms have turned their backs on me. Good fortune has its friends, and ill fortune its enemies! What will I do? Who will advise me? No one. I'm sure if I wanted to drown myself I could find someone to tie a stone around my neck. Come on now! God's in his heaven. Justice and innocence should count for something. I want to talk this over with the monsignor from Ravenna.[126] There aren't many like him at court. He's sure to give me the help and advice I need.

Scene ii.
(*Ercolano, drunk, and Togna*)

TOGNA: I'm standing here at the door waiting to see if that fool husband of mine comes back. I'd like to break his leg. It's night already but he hasn't come. This must be him now.
ERCOLANO: "Sh . . . show . . . show me the wa . . . wa . . . way to go ho . . . ho . . . home . . . ." Oh, the wind . . . windows are dancing. Ha, ha, ha! To . . . Togna, ho . . . hold me so I don't fa . . . fall in the Ti . . . Ti . . . Tiber. Ha, ha, ha!

TOGNA: I wish to God you would. It might water all that wine you've drunk, you old fool.
ERCOLANO: I'm no . . . not drunk. No, I'm a . . . asleep. The Cu . . . Cu . . . Culiseum is on my bed. Take me upstairs, qui . . . quick. I could sleep through the trumpets on Judgment Day.
TOGNA: Go on up, you pig! I'd like to tear you to pieces.

Scene iii.
(Messer Maco and Master Andrea)

MESSER MACO: Is this really me, Master?
MASTER ANDREA: If only it weren't.
MESSER MACO: Nonsense, I say. I want to screw her, I tell you!
MASTER ANDREA: Take it easy!
MESSER MACO: You'll have to take a sword to me! Christ, but I want to screw her!
MASTER ANDREA: Slow down! Here's the door. [*Knocks*]
MESSER MACO: Knock harder! Open up, by the body of . . .

Scene iv.
(Biasina, a maid, Master Andrea, and Messer Maco)

BIASINA: Who's there?
MESSER MACO: Me! It's me! I want to come up and sleep with the lady!
BIASINA: She's got company.
MESSER MACO: Send him away. Otherwise, you fucking cow . . .
BIASINA: What a boor! That's not the way a gentleman talks.
MASTER ANDREA: Open up, Biasina; don't let the gentleman here get angry.
BIASINA: One of yours, eh, you old goat you? I'll pull the latch. Come on in.
MESSER MACO: Well, you finally opened, did you, old shitface Marfisa?[127]

Scene v.
(Ercolano, alone, wearing his wife's clothes)

ERCOLANO: The bitch! The bitch! I should give her back to her brothers! I've caught her this time, the slut! Poor as I am,

I've never made her go without anything for lack of money. I'll find her if I have to run around all night, and then I'll cut her throat. Oh! Oh! Oh! I hadn't noticed till now, but those were *her* clothes at the foot of the bed. Did she leave the house in my clothes? You run away dressed as a man, and I chase you dressed as a woman! I'll go this way! No, this way! I'd better take the street through Borgo Vecchio — or maybe Santo Spirito — I'd be sure to get my hands on her in the Camposanto.[128] But she must have gone down this way, because she went out the back door.

Scene vi.

(Parabolano and Rosso)

PARABOLANO: It's a disagreeable feeling, this waiting!
ROSSO: Especially when hunger's gnawing away at us.
PARABOLANO: Quiet. One ... two ...
ROSSO: You think every bell you hear is a clock. That's Madam Onesta's funeral bell, and you're counting the hours! But listen: one ... two ... three ... four ... and a quarter. Your appetite will be looked after, and that rascal Lord Cupid ...
PARABOLANO: I've still got a year to wait!
ROSSO: Let's say two. As for me, I'm not going to stay out here in the open any longer. The wind's killing me, and I sure don't go for the idea of getting sick. Bloody women! Why aren't you content with money? That's what keeps everyone else going.
PARABOLANO: Let's go inside. I want you healthy, Rosso old fellow.

Scene vii.

(Valerio, alone)

VALERIO: Messer Gabriele Cesano and Messer Ioanni Tomaso Manfredi are certainly right to praise this Bishop of Cremona.[129] He's even kinder than everyone says he is. I told him my troubles and money was the least of what he offered me. It's a pity he's a priest and lives in this infernal court. Of the thousands you'll see there, there are only a couple of good ones: Ravenna and the most reverend Datario.[130] As for the others, take one look and then pass them by.[131] O court, how much more cruel you are than hell! It's true! Hell punishes vices but you revere, you adore them. But this isn't doing me any good. I must find my master. I'll find him walking by himself. I know where to look for him. I'll speak to him before I go to sleep and find out the cause of my troubles.

Scene viii.
(Master Andrea and Zoppino)

MASTER ANDREA: Zoppino, I'm tired of this joke. This guy is stupidity incarnate, and he's no fun any more. Let's jump him though — but first let's exchange our cloaks.

ZOPPINO: Here, give me yours, and you take mine.

MASTER ANDREA: Once we've thrown him out of the house we'll sleep with Camilla. [Knocks] Open up there! Ah! You've had it, you cheat! Coward! Lout! Stay where you are!

Scene ix.
(Messer Maco, in his nightshirt, throwing himself out a window)

MESSER MACO: Help! My ass is wounded! I've got a hole in my ass! The street! Run! I'm finished! But where am I running to? Where's the house? Oh dear! Oh dear!

Scene x.
(Parabolano and Rosso)

PARABOLANO: What was that noise?

ROSSO: Just someone partying.

PARABOLANO: Is it eleven o'clock yet?

ROSSO: What's the matter? Why are you so pale?

PARABOLANO: I'm pale on the outside because of the fires within.

ROSSO [aside]: You'll put your fires right out, you bastard.

PARABOLANO: I'm afraid that when I'm with her I won't be able to say a word.

ROSSO: No, no — you've got to chatter like a marketplace.

PARABOLANO: When one has a sensitive nature, Love steals away one's boldness.

ROSSO: Piss on Love! A man who's afraid to speak to a woman is a fool. Here's Aloigia, running like a thief.
PARABOLANO: Dear, dear!
ROSSO: What the devil's wrong?
PARABOLANO: I'm afraid that . . .

Scene xi.
(*Aloigia, Parabolano, and Rosso*)

ALOIGIA: Sir, Laura is in the house of your servant Aloigia (thanks to me), and she's waiting there for you, timid as can be. Do keep your word, sir, and this first time don't try to see her against her will. She's so bashful she'd die. Do what you have to do quickly, because although her husband has gone to one of his farmhouses, he sometimes comes back at night, and that'd be the ruin of her.
PARABOLANO: I'll do nothing to offend her. I'd rather pluck my eyes from their sockets.
ALOIGIA: Well, you take a little walk, and then go into my house.

Scene xii.
Parabolano and Rosso

PARABOLANO: O blessed night! You are dearer to me than the miraculous face of God to the pure in heart. O my bounteous star, which of my merits led you to bestow such a treasure upon me? O my faithful servant, how obliged I am to you!
ROSSO [*aside*]: That's the way: a little praise for me.
PARABOLANO: O angelic beauty of brow, of breast, of hands, soon I'll be your only possessor. O gentle lips, where Love distils the sweetest ambrosia, allow me, all fire as I am, to dip my own unworthy lips in your sweetness. O goddess, will you with your tranquil light illume the chamber, so that I may see her on whom my life and death depends?
ROSSO: An impressive prologue!
PARABOLANO: Isn't this what I'm supposed to do? Praise my mistress and the heavens for giving me such a gift?
ROSSO: Not as far as I'm concerned. I hate women like wine hates water.

Scene xiii.
(Aloigia, Parabolano, and Rosso)

ALOIGIA: Hush, sir. Come along quietly. Give me your hand.

PARABOLANO: Oh, God! How very, very thankful I am, Aloigia and Rosso!

ROSSO [*alone*]: Go on, eat a bit of that rotten meat you give us poor servants all year long. You crook! Wouldn't it be nice if some cutthroat was waiting in there to chop you up in a thousand pieces; then for a change you'd be the one who's treated like a dog!

Scene xiv.
(Aloigia and Rosso)

ALOIGIA: He's in the room with her, and he's roaring like a stallion that's just caught sight of the mares. He sighs and he weeps. And his bows! He makes more bows to her than the Spanish do in the Seggio Capuano.[132] He's promising to make her duchess of Magliana or Campo Salino.[133]

ROSSO: If I liked women, I'd have done what the lords do, and had a taste of her beforehand. But tell me, seriously: how many of these acts of mercy do you perform in the average year? Not that the bastards don't deserve even worse.

ALOIGIA: Thousands. I'd be hard put to find a Roman woman for every fool who wants one. Every peasant who gets a bit dolled up thinks he's a monsignor, and right away he wants me to bring him some high-born ladies. I give them bakers' wives to satisfy their appetites, and they pay me as if they were queens, the stupid fools. But what's on your mind?

ROSSO: I'm thinking that tomorrow I'll be escaping from the servants' mess—if he doesn't get wind of this little caper. And even if he does, what could happen? I can face it. I know I deserve to hang for the terrible thing I'm doing to my master, but I don't think about it.

ALOIGIA: What an awful man!

ROSSO: The only thing I've ever been afraid of is the servants' mess.

ALOIGIA: A big fellow like you, scared of the servants' mess?

ROSSO: If you could see the table all set up, and then had to eat the food that was on it, you'd be frightened to death yourself.

ALOIGIA: I've never happened to see one.

ROSSO: The moment you set foot inside, it doesn't matter whose it is, you find yourself in a cavern so dark it'd make a morgue seem cheery. In the heat of the summer it's boiling, and in winter the words freeze in your mouth. The stink's so fierce it'd take the smell from a civet cat. That's where the plague comes from, nowhere else! Shut up the servants' messes, and presto! Rome's cured of the plague.

ALOIGIA: Merciful heavens!

ROSSO: There are more colors on the tablecloth than on a painter's smock. It's washed in the pigs' tallow that's left over at night from the candles—although most of the time we eat in the dark. And the bread's as hard as enamel. You can never wash your hands or your face. We eat St. Luke's mother at every meal.

ALOIGIA: You eat Saints' flesh?

ROSSO: Even the crucified ones! No—when I said we eat St. Luke's mother I meant the way they paint them: he's an ox and his mother's a cow.

ALOIGIA: Ha, ha, ha!

ROSSO: That beef they feed us is older than creation, and it's cooked so badly, abstinence itself would lose its appetite.

ALOIGIA: They should be ashamed!

ROSSO: Morning and night always the same cow! The broth they make of it makes lye-water taste like sugar.

ALOIGIA: Aagh!

ROSSO: Don't throw up yet—there's worse! They always put kohlrabi and pumpkin in the soup—just when it's ready to be thrown out, I mean; otherwise, forget it. It's true, in place of fruit—as a refreshment—they give us a couple of chunks of buffalo cheese. But it sits in your stomach like a lump of glue that'd kill a statue.

ALOIGIA: Jesus!

ROSSO: Oh, and I'd forgotten about Lent. Listen to this: all through Lent they make us fast. You thought maybe they'd give us a treat in the morning? Four anchovies, or ten rotten sardines, and twenty-five cockles that would make hunger despair — but you're so exhausted that you take your fill. And a bowl of fava-beans without oil or salt. Then at night five bites of bread that would break the jaws of a satyr.

ALOIGIA: Oh, oh, oh, oh! That's terrible!

ROSSO: Then summer comes, and a man craves some place that's nice and cool. You go into the servants' mess, and the heat jumps up at you — it rises out of the filthy pile of bones, which is all covered with flies. It would frighten away rage, let alone appetite. How about a little refreshment? Some wine perhaps? Take it from me — a dose of medicine would be less disgusting. The wine is watered down with lukewarm water that's been sitting all day in a copper vat. I think it's the smell of the vat that refreshes you the most.

ALOIGIA: Filthy scoundrels!

ROSSO: Once in a hundred years there's a banquet, and the leftovers — things like chicken necks, and feet, and heads, stuff like that — they pass along to us, but by the time they get to us they've been through so many hands they're as dirty as Giuliano Leni's neckband.[134] Now here's the good news: our elegant and graceful servers are full of ringworm and syphilis! They wouldn't wash their hands if the Tiber was after them. You want to know how badly off we are? The walls are always weeping, as if they pitied the misery of those who eat there.

ALOIGIA: No wonder you're afraid of the servants' mess — you've got a thousand good reasons.

ROSSO: On Fridays and Saturdays it's always rotten eggs, and they're as stingy with them as if they'd just been laid. But what really makes us curse God is the way the butler treats us. We've hardly finished the last mouthful when he chases us away, banging away with his staff just for spite. We'd like to finish off the meal with a little conversation — since it's impossible to do it with the food — but he never lets us.

ALOIGIA: And everyone comes running to Rome to make courtiers of themselves, eh? Oh, it's cruel! And what's that? Oh, no! This is terrible! We're done for! Listen to the racket coming from my house! I was afraid this would happen! Oh dear, dear, dear! We're ruined! I'll go see what's going on.

Scene xv.
(Rosso, alone)

ROSSO: I'm done for. Throw me on the junk-pile. Where can I go where he can't get at me? Listen to that noise! He's going to kill both the baker's wife and the bawd. I've got to do something!

Scene xvi.
(Parabolano, alone)

PARABOLANO: I'm the most humiliated person in the world! And it serves me right—I let myself be taken in by a bawd and a servant. And I probably laughed, didn't I, when they played that joke on Messer Filippo Adimari.[135] He was told at vespers that they'd found four bronze statues when they were digging the foundations of the house he's having built in Trastevere. He ran like a fool to see them, on foot, alone and in his nightshirt, and when he found there was nothing there, he must have felt after that joke the way I feel now after this one. And I gave Messer Marco Bracci the Florentine[136] a hard time because of that wax statuette he found under his pillow. It was Pietro Aretino who'd put it there. Thinking it was witchcraft, he had Lady Marticca[137] flogged—she'd slept with him that night, so he thought she must have been so much in love that she cast a spell on him. It was the same way with Messer Francesco Tornabuoni[138]—remember the fun I had when he drank ten different syrups because we'd convinced him he had the French disease? Who wouldn't laugh? Valerio, Valerio, what a mistake it was to drive you away—and where are you now? Now I realize he was one servant who could see the truth.

Scene xvii.
(Valerio and Parabolano)

VALERIO: Here he is, sir, your servant Valerio. Whether you intended it or not, I recognize myself in what you said. And I deplore my wretched fate and those terrible slanders that have, for no reason at all, disgraced me in your eyes.

PARABOLANO: It's love that's to blame, Valerio. I was too credulous. I'm not usually like that. Don't be angry with me.

VALERIO: That's the way you great gentlemen are, and that's what makes me angry. You're quick to believe flatterers and liars, but you'll dismiss a faithful, honest man from your favor without even hearing what the absent suspect has to say.

PARABOLANO: Please forgive me. I was tricked by Rosso, who led me here to enjoy a whore, instead of the Roman gentlewoman who's the queen of my life.

VALERIO: So! Because of someone like Rosso, with all his fast talk, a gentleman like you lets himself fall into the hands of a common bawd—I saw you coming out of her house just now. Rosso talked you into dismissing someone who has served you for so many years with unquestioning obedience. You should be ashamed—a gentleman like you, blinded to common sense by a foolish appetite, putting us all in the hands of a pimp, and taking every lie as gospel truth.

PARABOLANO: No more! I'm ashamed to be alive! I'd like to kill them, both the young woman and the old one who lives here.

VALERIO: You'd be piling shame on top of disgrace! On the contrary, I beg you, let her get out, and let's have a good laugh about how they put a new twist on an old trick. Then you can be the first to tell it and people will forget your juvenile behavior that much sooner.

PARABOLANO: That's wise advice. Wait for me here.

Scene xviii.
(Valerio, alone)

VALERIO: Didn't I guess it was Rosso's doing? In the end, all you can do is pray to Christ. Otherwise, anyone who puts you at the mercy of a great lady becomes the master of masters and he can do what he wants, as if he were the master himself.

Scene xix.
(Parabolano, Togna, Aloigia, and Valerio)

PARABOLANO: I see! When I was dreaming I let it slip that I had fallen in love, and Rosso became the author of my disgrace.

ALOIGIA: Yes, sir. I'm putting myself in your good hands, Your Lordship. I did wrong, but it was because I was too compassionate and good! Oooh!

PARABOLANO: What? You're crying? Good God, I must do something for you!

ALOIGIA: When I saw that you were so lovesick, I was afraid that an overdose of love would make you even sicker, and so I made up my mind.

VALERIO: By God, she deserves to be forgiven; it's her compassionate nature and her ingenuousness that gives her the strength of mind to do such clever things.

PARABOLANO: Ha, ha, ha! Am I the first one?

ALOIGIA: No sir.

PARABOLANO: Ha, ha! By God, I've changed my mind — I'm going to laugh at this silly prank and my own stupidity! Whatever happens to me, it serves me right. I shouldn't have come. And Aloigia did just what she was asked to.

VALERIO: Now you're showing some common sense! And you, madam, you're looking sad! You're a better person for having had your pleasure with such a great gentleman.

TOGNA: Alas! I've been betrayed! I was brought here by force, dressed in my husband's clothes!

ALOIGIA: You're not telling the truth.

Scene xx.

(Ercolano, Togna, Aloigia, Valerio, and Parabolano)

ERCOLANO: Aah! I found you, you bitch! Aah! You pig! Don't hold me back!

PARABOLANO: Stay where you are! Don't move! Stay back! You're dressed as a woman! Ha, ha, ha!

ERCOLANO: She's my wife! I want to punish her!

TOGNA: You're lying!

ERCOLANO: Aah, you slut! This is the way I present myself to you — a horned man! I, who serve Lorenzo Cybo[139] and all the cardinals of the palace!

TOGNA: So what? I still belong to you, don't I?

ERCOLANO: Let go of me! Don't hold me back! I want to cut her throat! Put horns on Ercolano, would you?

VALERIO: He's the palace baker! Ha, ha! Stay back! Keep still! Put that down!

PARABOLANO: If this story doesn't end in tragedy it will just blow over. Calm down, Ercolano, and you too, Togna—I'm in on this dance too. I'd like to see all discord resolved at my expense. I consider myself lucky I got out of this as well as I did—at least you're no worse than a baker's wife.

ERCOLANO: As long as she comes back to me, I'll forgive her.

TOGNA: And I'll do whatever the gentleman here wants.

Scene xxi.
(Parabolano, Messer Maco in a nightshirt, Valerio, Ercolano, and Aloigia)

MESSER MACO: The Spaniards! The Spaniards!

PARABOLANO: What's all this racket? What is it?

MESSER MACO: The Spaniards wounded me! Thieves! Animals! Scoundrels!

PARABOLANO: What's going on, Messer Maco? Are you completely unhinged?

MESSER MACO: The traitors made a hole in my ass with their swords!

VALERIO: Ha, ha, ha! What a story! It's like something out of Aesop or Orlando! Poggio[140] can pick up his jokes and retire.

PARABOLANO: Come on, speak up! What is it? You were chasing around like this earlier today!

MESSER MACO: I wish I had . . . I'll tell you: Master Andrea had made a new courtier out of me, the handsomest one in Rome. At first, the devil saw to it that my appearance was ruined. Then, the moment that happened, it pleased God to re-make me, and He did a good job of putting me back together again. Since I'd been re-made, I wanted to do things my way, as was only right. So I went to the house of a certain lady. I undressed to go to bed with her, to have a bit of fun. But the Spaniards tried to kill me, so I jumped out the window. I almost broke my legs, Sir, you know that?

VALERIO: It really is true—God looks after children and fools! So you were in bad shape, but then you found someone in Rome to fix you up?

MESSER MACO: Yes, sir, if it please you, sir.

VALERIO: You've had a lot more luck than good sense. Many a better man than you has come to Rome in excellent trim and gone back home broken down and ruined. They don't care what you are or who you are—all they do is spoil good men and ruin them forever.

PARABOLANO: Ha, ha! Let's take this fellow and his story home with us, Valerio, I want to get a bit more fun out of it. I laugh fit to burst when I hear funny stories like these. Tell Pattolo[141] the whole thing tomorrow. He's witty and well read—tell him I'd like him to make a comedy out of it.

VALERIO: I'd be glad to. Madame Aloigia, come inside. This gentleman wants to be our friend in any way he can.

ALOIGIA: Your Lordship's servant. I'll see that he's satisfied.

VALERIO: And you, Messer Ercolana's wife, go inside with Aloigia. As for you, Ercolano, make the best of things. And keep your horns *invisibilium*.* These days the greatest gentlemen have them. If you knew your history, you'd remember that horns come from heaven—Moses wore them, and everyone could see them. Even the moon has horns and it's still in the sky. Oxen have horns and look at how much good they do with their plowing. It was because of the horn on his forehead that the horse Bucephalus was so dear to Alexander. And isn't it the horn the unicorn wears on his brow as protection against poison that makes him so precious? Finally, aren't the coats of arms of the Soderini[142] and Santa Maria in Portico[143] all horns? So keep them as marks of honor—as a crest. And remember how women with two beautiful horns found husbands for themselves, because, as I mentioned, Almighty God adorned the head of Moses with them, and he was the greatest friend He had in all of the Old Testament.

ERCOLANO: I don't know about all that. I wouldn't care if they all came from Limbo. I know a few noblemen who have some that are longer than a stag's. And I know this too: poor and in disgrace as you see me here now, I've given horns to a dozen others. As far as this one's concerned I'll leave it to my children to avenge it. Now, if you don't mind, I'll go inside.

---

*'invisible'

PARABOLANO: And you, Messer Maco, it's too risky to let you loose among women. They're the ruin of the world, and they know more about it than the schools of law do. A pillar can hold up a column for a thousand years, but a woman would try its patience. You come inside as well. I'll have your clothes returned to you tomorrow morning. Now be sensible, or those wicked women will drive you crazy.

MESSER MACO: I'll keep my wits about me as far as those bitches are concerned. Now that I'm a courtier, I've got to make a name for myself.

VALERIO: Well now, since I'm a lot happier than I thought I'd be, let's have a good laugh to finish off the evening.

My friends, if this story's taken too long, I want to remind you that everything takes too long in Rome. If you didn't like it, I'm glad to say it wasn't me who asked you to come here. If you wait around till next year, you're sure to hear a funnier one, but if you're in a hurry, see you at the Ponte Sisto.[144]

FINIS

Textual Annotations

1 Messer Mario was probably Mario de' Prevaschi, or Mario Perusco, a fiscal lawyer in the service of Pope Leo X, born in Perugia; he was one of the investigating judges in the trial against Cardinal Petrucci (see below, note 8).
2 Francesco [or "Chechoto"] de Castiglione Ligure was a tailor who had a shop on St. Peter's square and was well known for his practices in astrology. Pope Leo X gave him a monthly pension. He is also mentioned by Berni, a prominent writer of burlesque verse.
3 Lorenzo Luti was a painter, probably the same one mentioned by Mastro Andrea in a letter to Aretino (*Pasquinate* 164).
4 Beatrice de Bonis was a Roman prostitute, registered in the census of 1526 as living in the Ponte quarter, near the Albergo dell'Orso. She is the protagonist of the *Lamento della cortigiana ferrarese* (quoted by Aretino in *Sei giornate* 127, 210).
5 In 1300, Pope Boniface VIII (ca. 1235–1303) instituted the jubilee, which was to last for a year and was to be repeated every 100 years. During this period the pope grants plenary indulgences to all the faithful who make a pilgrimage to Rome, or who perform acts of equal merit. The interval between jubilee years was later changed to 25 years.
6 Girolamo Beltramo was a Jew of Spanish origin who converted to Christianity and made a fortune as a usurer. He lived in the Parione district and was protected by Pope Leo X. Berni refers to him as a clever card player.

7 Text has *Go look in Maremma*, which refers not to the region in Tuscany, but to a proverbial faraway place.
8 Battista da Vercelli was a well-known doctor. Under Leo X, those responsible for the conspiracy instigated by Cardinal Alfonso Petrucci (1517) were tried and condemned. A great impression was made by the execution by hanging of one of Petrucci's men-at-arms, Pocointesta Pocointesti, whose body was hung by the battlements of the Tordiona castle the morning of 6 June 1517, and an even greater one by the death by drawing and quartering of Marco Antonio Nino, Petrucci's steward, and Battista da Vercelli, who had taken on the task of poisoning the Pope.
9 Text uses the Latin phrase, *el tal è agens* [the doer], *el tal è patiens* [the receiver].
10 Francesco Armellini Medici (1470–1528) was born in either Perugia or Fossato. He inherited from his father the office of pontifical treasurer of the Marches, from which he amassed a huge fortune contracting excise taxes and selling livestock. In 1516 he was involved in a speculation in salt that almost ruined him and damaged the economy of the Apostolic Chamber. His new taxes on salt caused a popular revolt in Ancona in 1517. In the same year Pope Leo X made him a cardinal, and later a papal councillor and chamberlain. He continued in these duties also under the pontificate of Clement VII. He died in Rome in 1528. Hated by the poor, Armellini became the object of many *pasquinate* by Aretino and others.
11 The *volto santo*, the image of the face of Christ imprinted on the cloth with which Veronica wiped His face as He was carrying the cross. It is also called the "Veronica," and it is kept in the Vatican (St. John Lateran).
12 Apart from the taverns, these landmarks are, respectively, the Vatican; St. Peter's Basilica; St. Peter's Square; Castel Sant'Angelo; the large fountain at the head of Ponte Sisto near Via Giulia, built by Alberti, later moved across the river to a site near where the Trevi Fountain stands now; and the Church of Santa Caterina in the district of Regola.
13 The style of comedy in which Aretino wrote had established itself as a genre in the second half of the fifteenth century. It

combined characteristics of the *Commedia erudita* (which originated in Tuscany) and the street theater of Bergamo (which later developed into the *Commedia dell'Arte*). The *Commedia erudita* had a written text, for which the author was responsible, and often he also directed the performance, which took place at court; the Bergomask style, on the other hand, had only a *canovaccio* [an outline of the plot], and relied upon gestures, jokes, pranks, and the use of everyday language.

14 A parody of the imitators of Petrarch, who followed his superficial conventions but not his spirit.

15 Girolamo di Melchiorre de' Pandolfi (1464–1533) was a poet and adventurer, born at Cassio near Bologna, died in Rome. He was at the courts of two Medici popes, Leo X and of Clement VII (which accounts for his being called Cassio de' Medici). He wrote several books of verses and some saints' lives.

16 After the break-up of the Roman Empire, Italian peoples reverted back to their pre-Roman languages, which had, however, by then become variants of Latin. Dante, in the thirteenth century, realized that there was a problem as to which vernacular to use when writing in the vulgar tongue. In his treatise *De Vulgari eloquentia*, after discussing the origin of the languages, he comes to the conclusion that Florentine is the language to use, after incorporating words and expressions from other languages. At the beginning of the sixteenth century the language debate became very acute, involving some of the most prominent writers of the period, including Machiavelli, Bembo, Ariosto, Castiglione, and Speroni. During the Spanish and Austrian domination the debate subsided, but it came to the fore again after the *Risorgimento*. The solution reached today echoes that of Dante.

17 Pier Giovanni Cinotto was a poet and gentleman from Bologna. A famous prankster, he was welcomed at the court of Leo X.

18 Giovanni de' Medici (1475–1521), the second son of Lorenzo the Magnificent, was destined to the priesthood from childhood. In 1489 Pope Innocent VIII promised to make him a cardinal. Very shrewd and charming, he commended himself

to Pope Julius II, who placed him in positions of responsibility, in which he was very successful. In 1513, after Julius's death, he was elected pope and took the name Leo X. He held a lavish court and offered hospitality to men of letters, scholars, and agents who added to his collection of classical manuscripts. He continued some of the works started by Julius II, such as the building of the new St. Peter's and the decoration of the *stanze* by Raphael, and was an enthusiastic supporter of the arts in general.

19 Aretino mentions this person in Act I of *The Hypocrite* as well, but we have not been able to find out anything about him. The context implies that he was a well-known criminal.

20 The punishment named in the text is the *strappado*; it consisted of being tied with a rope at the thorax and dropped from a height until the rope brought the victim's fall to a violent and painful stop.

21 At the beginning of the sixteenth century the remains of a group of Greek marble statues from the third century B.C. were unearthed. The best-preserved example, apparently representing a Greek hero, was placed on a pedestal at the corner where Palazzo Orsini (today Palazzo Braschi) stands. The Roman people called it *Pasquino*. It is not clear where the name originated. Some say it was the name of a teacher who lived in the neighbourhood, others that it was the name of a tailor, still others that it was so called because it had been unearthed at Easter time (*Pasqua*). Soon Pasquino became very famous, almost a living character. The reason was this: almost every morning, writings in verse or prose satirizing the papal court or prominent nobles, in both Latin and Italian, would be found on the pedestal or on the back of the statue itself. These became known as *pasquinate*. These anonymous satires were crude and violent, and often led to lengthy polemics and fights. The author of some of the most violent and cruel *pasquinate* was Aretino himself.

22 For the ancients, Parnassus, a mountain in central Greece, was the home of Apollo, god of beauty, light, and poetry, and of the Muses. The Muses (and their respective jurisdictions) were Calliope (epic poetry); Clio (history); Erato (lyric poetry); Euterpe (music); Melpomene (tragedy); Polyhymnia

TEXTUAL ANNOTATIONS

(religious music); Terpsichore (dance); Thalia (comedy); and Urania (astronomy).

23 St. Francis of Assisi (ca. 1182–1226) was the son of Pietro Bernardone, a merchant. After a dissipated youth he renounced all his worldly goods, made a vow of absolute poverty, and started preaching poverty, humility, and charity. He founded the three Franciscan orders. In 1224 he received the stigmata on Mount Verna. He died at the Porziuncola, near Assisi. With St. Catherine of Siena he is considered the patron saint of Italy.

24 Mainaldo was a Mantuan antique dealer and jeweller. Aretino satirized him often and played many cruel jokes on him.

25 Cosimo Baraballo (1460–1516), also called Archipoeta, was a "papal baffoon, famous for his burlesque crowning on the Capitoline Hill, toward which he was led on the elephant Annone as people shouted *lazzi* [quips, jokes] and let fly a torrent of rotten fruit; the strange triumphal cortege provoked the immoderate laughter of the Pope, who was watching the hubbub from a *loggia*" (Del Vita, 999). Because of this "crowning," Aretino satirizes him in *pasquinate* and in the *Testamento dell'elefante*. He is also referred to by Ariosto under the name "Boraballe."

26 A *podestà* was the head of a medieval commune (city state); he was responsible for justice and for leading the army in war. Appointed, for a limited period of time, by the Holy Roman Emperor, he was not allowed to be a citizen of the town that he administered. The position of *podestà* was restored during the Fascist regime. It was equivalent to the position of mayor, and, as in the medieval period, the appointment was made from outside, by the central government.

27 Text uses Latin at this point: *tamen . . . ad un certum quid*.

28 Giovanni Battista Manenti was a broker in Venice who became rich organizing lotteries. Aretino wrote him a letter and also mentions him in *Pasquinate romane*.

29 Mastro Andrea was a Venetian painter, well known in Rome during the pontificate of Julius II more for his pranks and jokes than for his art. He was a friend of Aretino, whose verses he would collect. His death at the hands of the Spaniards during the Sack of Rome (1527) was related to Aretino by

Sebastiano del Piombo in a letter. He is also a character in Aretino's *Trionfo della lussuria di maestro Pasquino* (Venice, 1537), a poem of four chapters in tercets, featuring the most famous prostitutes of Rome. Mastro Andrea himself wrote *Il Purgatorio delle Cortigiane*, which was reprinted many times (the *Purgatori* is the Roman hospital of S. Giacomo, also called *degl'Incurabili*, where many prostitutes suffering from syphilis ended up). Mastro Andrea is also mentioned by Aretino in *Sei giornate*.

30 See note 25. The elephant had been donated to Pope Leo X by King Emanuele of Portugal and for a long time served as entertainment for the whole court. In 1516 Aretino wrote *Il testamento dell'elefante* [The Elephant's Will], a marvellous satire of the Rome of Leo X.

31 Accursio and Serapica were well-known clowns and guzzlers in the Roman court. Accursio (Francesco da Cazaniga, from Milan) was a courtier of both Julius II and Leo X; when he first came to Rome he became a bailiff of the goldsmith Caradosso. Aretino mentions him also in *Sei giornate*, 195, and in *Ragionamento delle corti*, 42. Serapica, Giovanni Lazzaro de Magistris, born in l'Aquila, rose from tending dogs and falcons at the papal court to the role of secret chamberlain to Leo X, and also acquired considerable wealth by stealing on the job. After the death of the Pope he was brought to justice and condemned by Pope Adrian VI. He is also mentioned in several of Aretino's letters and in *Sei giornate*, 195. Caradosso is Cristoforo di Giovanni Maffeo Foppa, a goldsmith and medal-maker; he was born in Mondonico (Como) in 1452, worked in Milan in the service of Ludovico il Moro, and in 1505 moved to Rome, where he died in 1527.

32 The cities that claimed to be Homer's birthplace were Smyrna, Chios, Cumae, Pilo, Ithaca, Argos, and Athens.

33 Matelica is a town in the Marches, in the province of Macerata, known for its fur and for its mechanical and food industries.

34 Gian Pietro Carafa (1476–1559) became Bishop of Chieti in 1506. After the Sack of Rome he found refuge in Venice. He founded the monastic order of the Teatini, and in 1555 was elected pope, taking the name Paul IV. In 1557 he published the first Index of forbidden books. While Aretino was in

Rome he had satirized Carafa in his *pasquinate* and *pronostici*, but his attitude toward him changed.

35 Giannozzo Pandolfini, a Florentine priest who became a prelate at the court of Leo X, was Bishop of Troja, in the province of Foggia, from 1484 to 1514. He died in 1525. See Aretino, *Sei giornate*, 195.

36 Siena had at least nine public fountains. The Fonte Becci was built in 1218 and most of the others about the same time. The Fonte Branda, built before 1193 and rebuilt several times, is the most famous because of the water's abundance and its particular qualities. The piazza is the famous Piazza del Campo, built in the shape of a shell, at the top of which is Fonte Gaja (1343), sculpted in 1419 by Jacopo della Quercia, and at the bottom the magnificent Palazzo della Signoria (started in 1284).

37 The allusion here is to an episode that occurred in 1462. A Sienese bought a woodpecker, convinced that it was a parrot, and gave it to Pope Pius II (Enea Silvio Piccolomini, 1405–1464), who was passing through Corsignano, his native town. Luigi Pulci (1432–84) mentions this episode in his work *Morgante*, 14: 53 1–5 as an example of the stupidity of the Sienese.

38 *Verbum caro* is another term for the Veronica; see note 11.

39 See note 5.

40 See note 2.

41 Baccano, Storta, and Tre Capanne are three localities with bad reputations on the outskirts of the city.

42 S.P.Q.R. is the abbreviation for *Senatus Populus Que Romanus* [the Senate and the Roman People]. These initials are found on public works everywhere in Rome.

43 The titles refer, respectively, to the truce between Pope and the Emperor ratified by the peace of Madrid in 1526; the capture of Francis I following the battle of Pavia, 24 February 1525; The Reform of the Court, a work by Carafa (see note 34); *The Caprices*, by Mariano Fetti (1460 [Florence]–1531 [Rome]), the most famous clown in the courts of Pope Adrian VI and Pope Clement VII, one of the monks of the Papal Seal, and the Abbot in charge of the Dominican convent of San Silvestro in the Quirinale district; *La Caretta* (*The Cart*), probably *Lamento di una cortigiana ferrarese*, first attributed to Mastro Andrea,

but later claimed by Aretino as his own work; no information is available on *Il Cortigiano falito*.

44 A *baiocco* is a Roman copper coin of little value, in use in the papal states until 1866. The expression *non valere un baiocco* means "not worth much," and is often applied to a person.

45 These lines are taken from the *Lamento di una cortigiana ferrarese*, but are based on a popular song. Madrema-non-vuole [Momma-Doesn't-Want-Me-To] and Lorenzina were names by which two prominent prostitutes were known.

46 Giulio de' Medici, the future Pope Clement VII, was named Prior of Capua by his second cousin, Pope Leo X, in 1514.

47 The king of Cyprus is probably Eugenio di Lusignano, pretender to the throne of Cyprus; Costantino Comneno, Duke of Acaia and Prince of Macedonia, was named governor of Fano by Leo X in 1516; there is no such town as Fiossa, although a number have spellings that are similar.

48 Raphael was a usurer in the Borgo district.

49 Romanello was a Jewish second-hand dealer who had his shop in the Borgo and who furnished stockings to the court of Leo X.

50 Adrian Florensz of Utrecht, the last non-Italian pope before John Paul II, took the name Adrian VI and was pope from 1522 to 1523. He was responsible for the internal reform of the Church.

51 *La gatta di Massino* is an expression applied to a person who pretends not to see anything.

52 Mangiaguerra is a dark, almost black, concentrated wine.

53 Gian Maria Giudeo, lord of the manor of Verrucchio (ancient castle of the Malatesta family in Romagna) and also lord of the Scorticata (today Torriana), was a famous lutenist in the court of Leo X; his brother Baldessar and his son Camillo were also well-known musicians. They may have been of Germanic origin.

54 Text uses the Latin phrase *e non fare una leva eius*, to run away.

55 The Ponte Sisto was a bridge in the Arenula district; the Arenula had a very bad reputation as a meeting place for prostitutes, skid-row tramps, and other riff-raff. Someone "sent to Ponte Sisto," then, would have been dismissed, and thus condemned to destitution.

TEXTUAL ANNOTATIONS 149

56 These are all places in Florence: Porta Pinti is now known as Porta Roma; San Pietro Gattolini is a church in Via Romana; Borgo a la Noce is a district near the Church of San Lorenzo.
57 The Colonnas and the Ursini were the two most powerful Roman families at this time.
58 San Gregorio's masses are masses for the dead.
59 See note 2.
60 The Barco is the quarry of travertine marble in Via Tiburtina, near Ponte Lucano; Botte di Termine is a water cistern within the Diocletian Baths, not far from the Fontanone dell'Acqua Felice; the arches are the triumphal arches of the emperors; Testaccio has not been identified.
61 See note 21.
62 A rebec is a medieval instrument with three strings, played with a bow, favored by troubadours.
63 Ludovico Arrighi, from Vicenza, and Lutizio di Bartolomeo d' Rutelli (who died in 1527) were engravers and printers of the first half of the sixteenth century. They formed a company in 1524, at which time they published two poems by Aretino, *Canzone in lode di papa Clemente* VII and *Canzone in lode del Datario*.
64 Pope Innocent VIII started the building of Palazzo Belvedere in the Vatican, but it was Pope Julius II who conceived the famous courtyard and the large conch (a semi-circular niche surmounted by a half-dome), which were designed and built by Bramante.
65 Brandino and the Morro de' Nobili were buffoons and parasites at the court of Leo X. Domenico Brandino, Cavalier of Rodi, was from Pisa, Giovan Battista de' Nobili, known as "the Moor," from Florence.
66 Borgo Vecchio was the old Via Santa, which led to the Vatican before Pope Alexander VI built Via Alessandrina (known as Borgo Nuovo); Corte Savella was a court of law; Torre di Nona (now known as Tordinona) was a jail; for Ponte Sisto see note 55; Dietro Banchi, or Banchi Vecchi, near Via Calabraga, now called Via Cellini (Benvenuto Cellini lived there), was well known at the time of Aretino as a quarter frequented by prostitutes.

67 An enormous bronze pine cone was placed in St. Peter's Square during the medieval period, and then in the courtyard of Palazzo Belvedere in the Vatican; "the ship" is Giotto's mosaic of the "Navicella" in the portico of St. Peter's Basilica; Camposanto, the Vatican cemetery, is now in Via Teutonica in the Vatican; the obelisk was moved from Nero's Circus to St. Peter's Square in 1586.
68 Leo X.
69 Alessio Caledonio was Bishop of Malfetta from 1508 until his death in 1517. Well known for his avarice, he was harshly satirized by Pasquino. He left his whole inheritance to Pope Leo X.
70 Ferdinando Ponzetta, a doctor and apostolic treasurer (1437–1527), succeeded Caledonio (see previous note) as Bishop of Malfetta in 1517, and Leo X made him a cardinal the same year.
71 The Strozzi Bank, near the Strozzi Palace, no longer exists; it was located where the Argentina Theater is now.
72 For San Gregorio's masses see note 58; St. Julian's paternosters: a prayer said to be useful for assuring hospitality and protection during travel.
73 The notion that witches and sorcerers gathered at the huge walnut tree at Benevento was very popular, especially during the Renaissance. The saying *sott'acqua e sotto vento sotto il noce di Benevento* [in rain and wind under the walnut tree of Benevento] is still current. In the late nineteenth century the liqueur producer, Alberti, based in Benevento, developed a liqueur that is said to rival the Benedictine, which he named *Strega* [witch], in recognition of the legend.
74 See note 4.
75 Capovacina may be either Liello di Rienzo Massienzo capo Vaccina, or Renzo Jacobacci, a Roman bravo. Parione is the district of Rome where Pasquino is found.
76 The fortress of San Leo, near Pesaro, was long thought to be impregnable — even Dante mentioned it (*Purgatory* 4: 25). Aretino may be referring to its conquest in 1502 by Cesare Borgia, or, fourteen years later, by Lorenzo de' Medici, Duke of Urbino.
77 Fata Morgana was the fairy sister of King Arthur in Arthurian romance; she also appears in Ariosto and Tasso.

TEXTUAL ANNOTATIONS 151

78 A *strambottino* is a poem, usually satirical or amorous, of eight eleven-syllable lines, in alternate rhymes. It became a very common musical composition.
79 Text has *carlini*. The *carlino* takes its name from Charles I of Anjou, King of Naples, who first had it minted in 1278. Made of gold or silver, and of varying value, it was coined in other Italian states up to the nineteenth century.
80 Astolfo was the famous English paladin in Ariosto's *Orlando furioso*, who flies to the moon on a winged horse, has Orlando's senses stored in vials, and brings them back to earth so that Orlando can regain his sanity and, of course, win the war.
81 Norcia is a town in Umbria, an agricultural and commercial center known for the production of salami and sausages; also the birthplace of St. Benedict and of St. Scolastica; its fortress was designed by Vignola. Todi is a town in Umbria that flourished under the Etruscans; it was the birthplace of the medieval poet Jacopone and is known for its marvellous Duomo, its churches and palaces, and its furniture industry; for Baccano, see note 41.
82 Marforio is a statue of a river god (perhaps that of the Tiber), so called because it was placed in Piazza Marforio (in 1592 it was moved to the Capitoline Museum). Roman satire made the god Pasquino's interlocutor in numerous burlesque dialogues.
83 The Sapienzia Capranica was the university in Piazza degli Orfanelli, in the Colonna district, founded in 1456–1457 by Cardinal Domenico Capranica; also called Sapienza Fermana so as not to be confused with the other university, la Sapienza Romana.
84 Strascino was the Sienese poet Niccolà Campani, a friend of Aretino.
85 See note 25.
86 The name Mescolone suggests a big fool who gets everything mixed up (*mescolare*: "to mix"; *-one*: a suffix, often derogatory, meaning "big").
87 He is referring to the old hospital of Santo Spirito in Sassia.
88 See note 66.

89 Orlando is the lover-hero in *Orlando Innamorato* (1483) by Matteo Maria Boiardo.
90 The market used to be held in the Piazza Navona, before the transformation in the Baroque period that made it one of the most beautiful piazzas in Rome.
91 A mangling of the name Parabolano; but Rapolano Terme is also the name of a town near Siena, known for its medicinal baths.
92 See note 43.
93 Benedetto Accolti, Jr. (1497–1549), nephew of Piero Accolti, Bishop of Ancona (1505), was made Archbishop of Ravenna and cardinal in 1527. He was an ecclesiastical writer, but more importantly, he was a powerful businessman. At first Aretino attacked him, but their relations became friendlier. Of a very violent temperament, he committed many crimes when he was the apostolic legate in Ancona in 1532. Because of this he was arrested by Pope Paul III and imprisoned in Castel Sant'Angelo. Here Aretino seems to be referring to an act of generosity toward Giovan Battista Ubaldini, a writer and man of letters and a friend of Accolti.
94 In Milan Francesco II Sforza was trying to free himself from Spanish domination; at Ferrara Alfonso I d'Este was trying to resume good relations with Charles V after the battle of Pavia; Naples for a while had been the object of a struggle between France and Spain; Francesco Maria delle Rovere, Duke of Urbino, was consolidating his control of the duchy after the attacks of Leo X.
95 Federico II Gonzaga (1500–1540) was Marquis and Duke of Mantua, Marquis of Monferrat. One of the most illustrious princes of the period and a protector of artists and writers, he helped Aretino several times. In 1519 he succeeded his father Francesco, fourth Marquis of Mantua, to whom Aretino refers in *Il Marescalco* IV, 5.
96 Pope Leo X and Pope Clement VII were second cousins.
97 Text has *Oe vorei prima una pernice che Beatrice*, with a play on the *pernice–Beatrice* rhyme, for which we have tried to find a counterpart in English. Beatrice Paregia was a well-known prostitute.
98 See note 45.

TEXTUAL ANNOTATIONS 153

99   Antonio Lelio was a satirical poet and author of *pasquinate*; he lived in the Parione district.
100 See note 28.
101 When Charles VIII of France (1470–1498), with the help of Ludovico il Moro, Duke of Milan (1452–1508), came to Italy and occupied the Kingdom of Naples (1494–1495), syphilis spread like wildfire — hence the name "French disease."
102 See note 10.
103 Perhaps this is Cesare De Gennato, to whom Aretino addressed a letter in 1540.
104 See note 66.
105 Priapus was the Greek god of fertility. In Rome he was also honored as the god of gardens. Here the allusion is to Maco, who yearns to have sexual intercourse.
106 The church is Santa Maria d'Aracoeli, on the Capitoline Hill.
107 It is possible that Tinca Martelli was a historical character, but certainly Captain Tinca, mentioned by many writers, including Ariosto in the comedy *Lena*, is an example of the *miles gloriosus*.
108 See note 53.
109 See note 16. The language controversy, especially in poetry, was one of Aretino's constant themes.
110 The medlar tree is very common in central and southern Italy. Its fruit is picked in late fall before the frost and put in hay to ripen. The reference here is to the bitter taste of the medlar if it is eaten before it is ripe.
111 Bartolomeo Colleoni (1400–1476) was a highly successful *condottiere* (leader of a troop of mercenaries) who was for most of his life in the service of the Republic of Venice. In 1445 he was made captain for life of the armies of the Republic. He was immortalized in a famous equestrian statue in Venice by Verrocchio (1435–1488). Aretino uses the spelling "Coglione" to call attention to the pun associated with the name — *coglione* means "testicle," and Colleoni used the image of a pair of testicles as his emblem. The Malatestas were one of the most powerful families of Renaissance Italy. Aretino seems to be referring to Sigismondo Pandolfo Malatesta (1417–68), *condottiere*, poet, student of antiquity, and munificent patron of

the arts, often considered the archetype of the Italian Renaissance prince.
112 See note 31.
113 The similarity between this name and the name that appears in Act II, scene 6 (see note 75) suggests that Aretino may be playing with the name of a Roman bravo, or perhaps more than one.
114 This is Rosso's version of Tivoli, a small village near Rome, which of course has no Duke; it is the site of the summer residences of the most affluent and powerful Romans, both ancient and modern, notably the Villa d'Este; famous for its waterfalls, Tivoli is situated on the Aniene River, and has supplied water for the fountains of Rome since ancient times.
115 Angelo de Cesis was a fiscal lawyer for Pope Julius II and Pope Leo X (d. 1528).
116 Velletri is a town of Volscian origin south of Rome, known for its wine and olive oil.
117 *Il mal mi preme e mi spaventa il peggio.* Petrarch, *Canzoniere* 244: 1.
118 Text has *potresti dare in un trentuno,* you could be taken by 31 men, one after the other. See *Sei Giornate* 73–75 and Glossary.
119 San Lorenzo Fuori le Mura ('outside the walls') was one of the churches that made money through the sale of indulgences during Lent.
120 When Ercolano says he is "from Corneto" (i.e., he wears horns [*corna*] on his head) or "from Cervia" (i.e., he is a male deer), he is saying that he wears the proverbial horns of a cuckold.
121 Ricordo means keepsake, souvenir.
122 This is a reference to the biblical story of the crow that Noah sent from the ark; it never came back.
123 Cristoforo Numalio, called Aracoeli (d. 1527), was General of the Order of the Minor Friars. He was made cardinal by Pope Leo X in 1517 with the title of St. Matthew, then transferred to Santa Maria d'Aracoeli.
124 See note 10.
125 The Chigi bank.
126 See note 93.
127 Marfisa is a character from the epic poems of the period.

TEXTUAL ANNOTATIONS 155

128 Borgo Vecchio: see note 66; Santo Spirito: see note 87; Camposanto: see note 67.
129 Gabriel Cesano was a man of letters from Pisa (1490–1568), to whom Claudio Tolomei dedicated *Il Cesano*; Joanni Tomasi Manfredi was an agent in Rome for the Duchess Eleonora of Urbino; Pietro Accolti, uncle of Benedetto, Jr. (see note 93), took the place of his nephew as Bishop of Cremona from 1524 to 1529.
130 For Ravenna, see note 93; Giovanni Matteo Giberti (1495–1543) was Bishop of Verona and datary of Pope Clement VII. He actively promoted the Catholic Reformation. His work *Constitutiones* was very influential in the formulation of the canons of the Council of Trent. Giberti tried to have Aretino killed because Aretino attacked him violently many times in his *pasquinate*.
131 This is an allusion to Dante's *Inferno* III:51.
132 According to Romano, the Seggio Capuano was one of the most ancient of the five *seggi* [seats] in which Neapolitan nobility had been grouped since the fourteenth century. Petrocchi, however, identifies it with a Neapolitan quarter near Porta Capuana, where poor people lived.
133 La Magliana and Campo Salino were papal possessions, the latter, known for its salt works, situated at the mouth of the Tiber River near Fiumicino.
134 Giuliano Leni was an astrologer and guzzler at the court of Pope Leo X. Of Florentine origin, he was a conclavist with Cardinal Orsini and a friend of the great architect Bramante (see note 64).
135 Filippo Adimari was a Florentine noble who came to Rome with Giulio de' Medici.
136 Marco Bracci was a Florentine gentleman at the court of Pope Leo X. Died in Rome, 1551.
137 Marticca was a Roman courtesan.
138 Francesco Tornabuoni was another Florentine nobleman brought to Rome by Pope Leo X.
139 Lorenzo Cybo (1500–1549), captain of the papal army, brother of Cardinal Innocenzo (who built the 2,000-seat theater in which Ariosto's *Suppositi* was performed in 1519), was Marquis of Massa and Count of Ferentillo. A nephew of Pope

Leo X, he followed his uncle's wish and married Ricciarda Malaspina, Marchioness of Massa, the mother of Giulio Cybo. The marriage, however, was a rocky one.

140 The famous humanist Poggio Bracciolini (1380–1459) was author of the *Facetiarum liber*.

141 The Florentine Bartolomeo Pattolo was a dilettante poet at the court of Pope Leo X, author of the *Orchessa*, scorned by his contemporaries, including Aretino.

142 Cardinal Francesco Soderini (1453–1524) was Bishop of Volterra and adversary of Pope Clement VII. He seems to have been involved in the conspiracy of Petrucci (see note 8).

143 Bernardo Dovizi da Bibbiena, a man of letters and a diplomat, was made cardinal by Pope Leo X, with the title Santa Maria in Portico. His coat of arms consisted of two cornucopias (horns of plenty) filled with flowers, in the form of a cross.

144 See note 55.

Carleton Renaissance Plays in Translation

This volume of the Carleton Renaissance Plays in Translation was produced using the TeX typesetting system, with Adobe Palatino PostScript fonts.